Norihiro Yagi won the 32nd Akatsuka Award for his debut work, *UNDEADMAN*, which appeared in *Monthly Shonen Jump* magazine and produced two sequels. His first serialized manga was his comedy *Angel Densetsu* (Angel Legend), which appeared in *Monthly Shonen Jump* from 1992 to 2000. His epic saga, *Claymore*, is running in *Monthly Jump Square* magazine.

In his spare time, Yagi enjoys things like the Japanese comedic duo Downtown, martial arts, games, driving, and hard rock music, but he doesn't consider these actual hobbies.

CLAYMORE VOL. 23
SHONEN JUMP ADVANCED Manga Edition

STORY AND ART BY
NORIHIRO YAGI

English Adaptation & Translation/John Werry
Touch-up Art & Lettering/Sabrina Heep
Design/Amy Martin
Editor/Megan Bates

Printed in the U.S.A.

Published by VIZ Media, LLC
P.O. Box 77010
San Francisco, CA 94107

10 9 8 7 6 5 4 3 2 1
First printing, October 2013

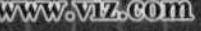

SHONEN JUMP ADVANCED Manga Edition

クレイモア

Claymore

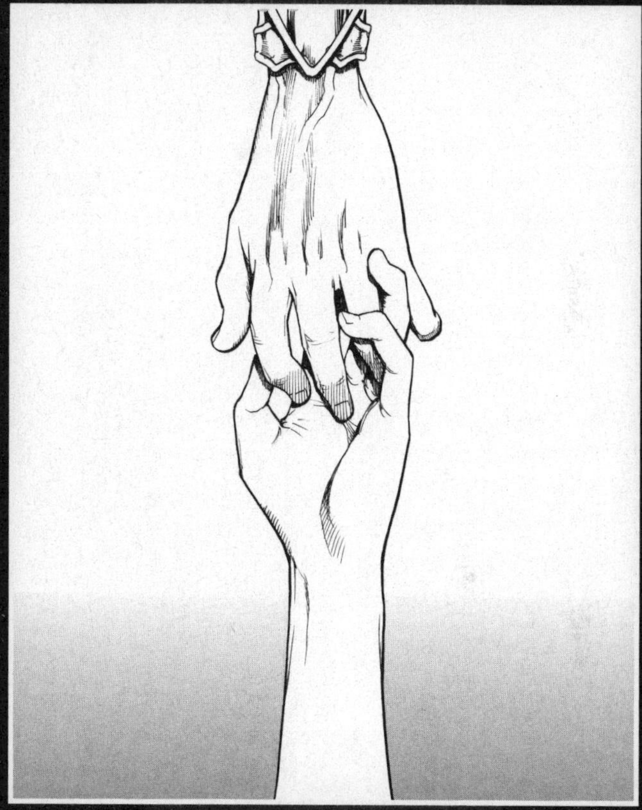

Vol. 23
Mark of the Warrior

Story and Art by Norihiro Yagi

To wipe out Warriors who have risen up in revolt, the Organization revives three former Warriors who were ranked Number One, but they awaken one after the other and become Abyssal Ones. After a dreadful battle, Raki appears before the Warriors...

The Story Thus Far
Creatures known as Yoma have long preyed on humans who were once powerless against their predators. But now mankin has developed female warriors who are half human and half monster, with silver eyes that can see the monsters' true form These warriors came to be calle Claymores after the immense broadswords that they carried.

クレイモア

Claymore

Vol. 23

CONTENTS

Scene 126: Claws and Fangs of the Abyss, Part 7

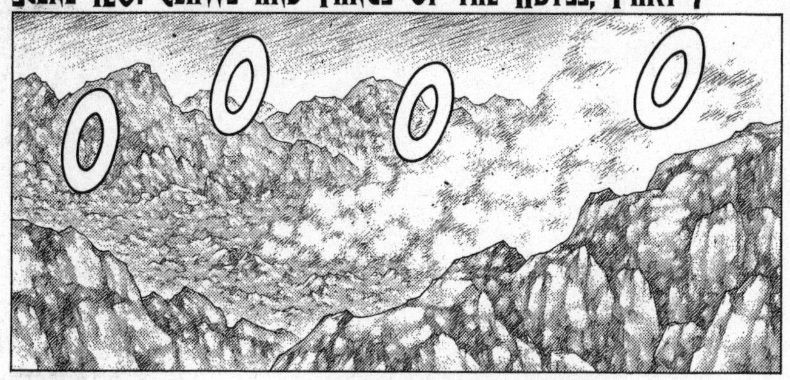

WELL ...
TOK
I DON'T KNOW WHAT YOUR STAKE IN THIS IS...
ZA
...BUT IF YOU'RE INTER-ESTED, I WILL SHOW YOU THE REAL THING.
DO YOU KNOW THE LOCATION ...
...OF HER ACTUAL BODY?
HEH HEH HEH...
HMM...

SCENE 126: CLAWS AND FANGS OF THE ABYSS, PART 7
THE ONLY THING THAT'S CLEAR IS THAT...
...WHILE HER LOCATION REMAINS AMBIGUOUS...
...THERE IS NOW THE DISTINCT POSSIBILITY OF FINDING HER.

GA SHA

DAMN! NO ONE HERE, EITHER!
JUST LIKE HE SAID, THIS PLACE IS EMPTY.

HUFF
HUFF

...
ARG ...

THE TWINS ASKED ME TO PROTECT THE TRAINEES.
WE FOUGHT OUR WAY THROUGH ANYONE WHO GOT IN OUR PATH.

READ THIS WAY

BUT THEN WE FELT A LARGE SHOCK...
...AND AT THE SAME TIME OUR PURSUERS SUDDENLY DISAPPEARED.

MIRIA ...
YEAH.

THE ORGANIZATION ABANDONED THIS PLACE...
...WHEN THE THREE ABYSSAL ONES APPEARED.

BUT WE SHOULD KEEP SEARCHING.
LET'S SPLIT UP.
IF YOU FIND ANYONE FROM THE ORGANIZATION, TAKE THEM DOWN.

WE CAN'T LET THIS CONTINUE.
I THINK THIS IS THE BEST WAY.

I'LL SEARCH DEEPER IN THIS DIRECTION.
DENEVE, GO EAST.
HELEN, YOU GO WEST.
ALL RIGHT.
I'M ON IT.

DA
DA

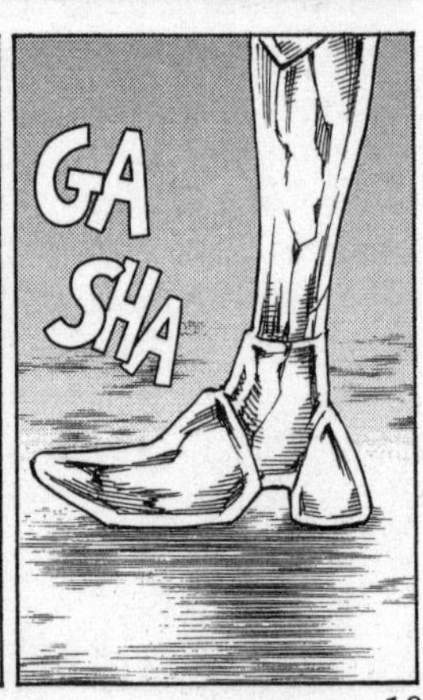
GA
SHA

GA
SHA
GA
SHA

GASHA

READ THIS WAY

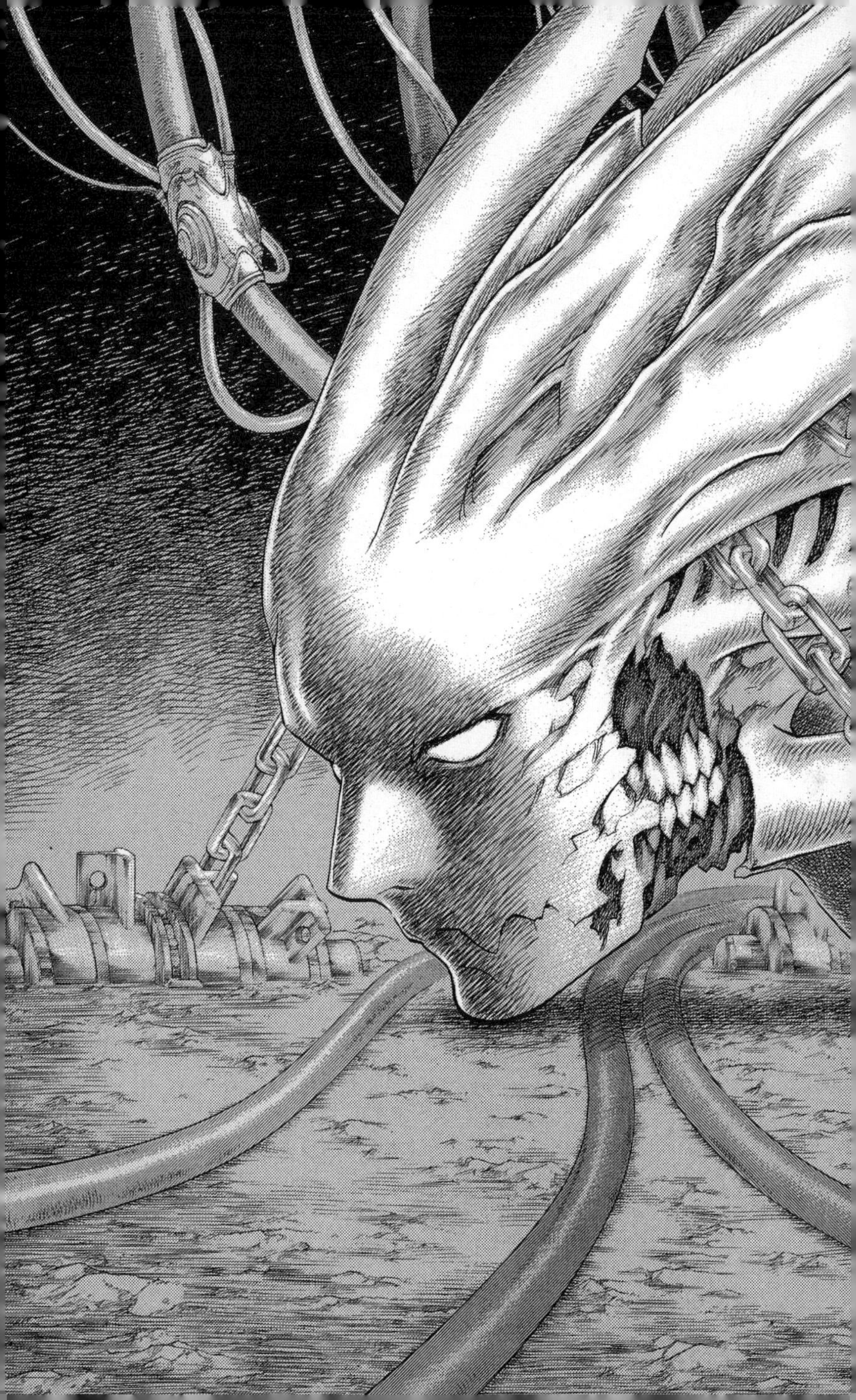

IS IT YOUR FIRST TIME SEEING THIS?
!
OR PERHAPS NOT...

THIS IS THE AWAKENED FORM OF AN ASARA-KAMU...
...A CLAN SAID TO BE DE-SCENDED FROM DRAGONS.

LIMT ...

TO BE EXACT, IT IS DIFFERENT FROM YOUR AWAKENING, BUT WE CALL IT THAT FOR CONVE-NIENCE.

LIKE YOURS, HOWEVER, THERE IS NO GOING BACK.

AND THAT ONE IS...
...THE ORIGINAL FORM.
EVEN SO, IT IS TWICE OUR SIZE.
THEY ARE ANDROGYNOUS AND LIVE ABOUT 200 YEARS.

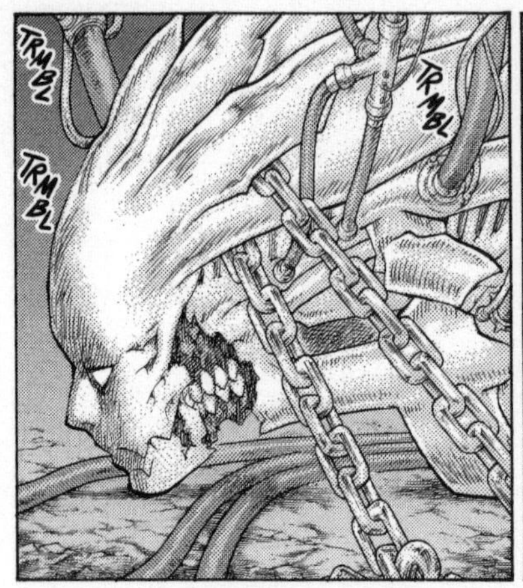
TRMBL
TRMBL
TRMBL

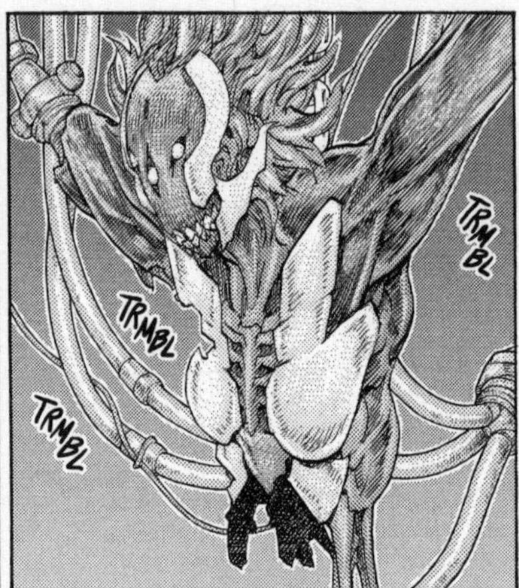
TRMBL
TRMBL
TRMBL

KEPT LIKE THIS...
...YET THEY'RE BOTH STILL ALIVE?

OF COURSE.
THERE WOULD BE NO POINT OTHER-WISE.
AFTER DEATH THIS SPECIES DECOM-POSES...
...AT AN UNBE-LIEVABLE RATE.

LITTLE BY LITTLE WE SCRAPE AWAY THEIR LIVING FLESH...
...AND FUSE THEM INTO SOMETHING NEW AND IMPERISHABLE.

THEN WE HAVE THAT SQUIRM-ING THING...
...FEED ON THE BRAIN OF A MEDIUM.

READ THIS WAY

AND THE RESULT ...
...IS YOMA.

I'VE KNOWN SINCE I SAW THIS PLACE NINE YEARS AGO...
...THAT YOMA DID NOT NATURALLY COME TO BE.
THE HOSTS CRAVE HUMAN ORGANS, WHICH THE ORGANIZATION USES FOR ITS OWN ADVANTAGE.
DUE TO ABUSE AND DEFORMATION, THEIR BODIES BREAK, SO THE PARASITE FINDS A NEW HOST.
THAT THEY EAT PEOPLE TO ADOPT THEIR APPEARANCE AND MEMORIES IS NONSENSE MADE UP BY THE ORGANIZATION.

ALL ALONG ...

...WE WARRIORS HAVE BEEN KILLING HUMANS.

THAT IS WHY...

...I WANTED TO CRUSH THIS PLACE ALONE.

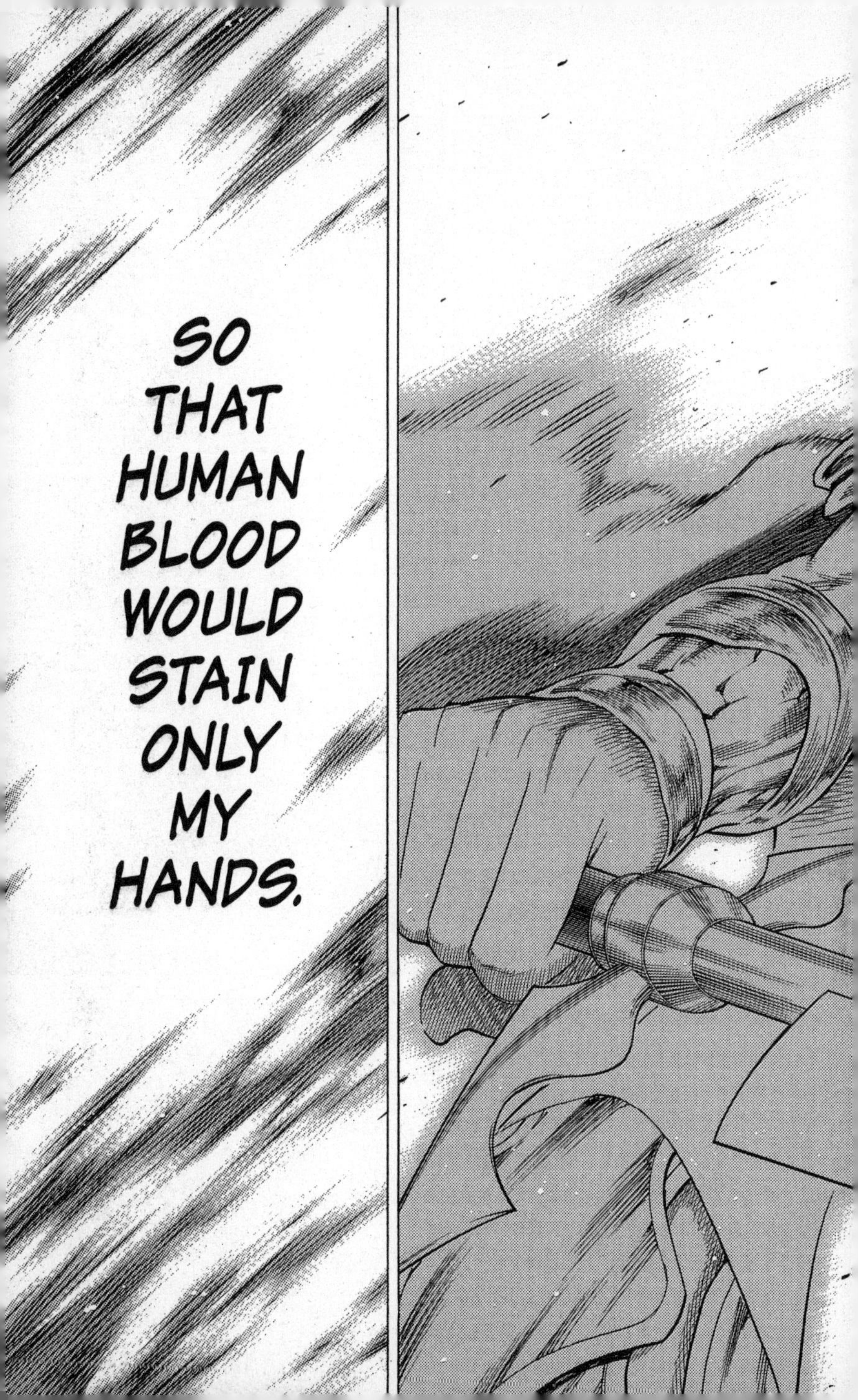
SO THAT HUMAN BLOOD WOULD STAIN ONLY MY HANDS.

GASH
GASH

BUSHAAA

GLUP
GLUP
GLUP

GLUP
GLUP
GLUP

READ
THIS
WAY

BOKO
BOKO
BOKO

GASHI

BOKO
BOKO
BOKO

DOSHAAAA

GASHA

MIRIA! THERE YOU ARE!
!

IT'S NO USE, MIRIA.
THERE'S NO ONE ANYWHERE.

!
!!

M...
MIRIA ...
WHAT'S THAT...?

IT'S THE HEAD OF LIMT, AN ORGANI-ZATION ELDER.
I FOUND HIM HIDING BELOW AND CUT OFF HIS HEAD.

READ THIS WAY

OH...
...

B...
BELOW ...?
THE ORGANIZATION WAS IN A PLACE LIKE THIS?

GA SHA
GA SHA

IF EVERYONE ELSE RAN AWAY...
...WHY DID LIMT STAY BELOW ALL ALONE?

I DON'T KNOW.
BUT HE WAS THE ORGANIZATION'S LEADER...
...SO HE WAS TO BLAME FOR THE REBELLION AND DEFEAT OF THE ORGANIZATION.

TO HIM IT WAS JUST ...
...A DIFFERENT PLACE TO DIE.

HUFF
HUFF
HUFF

YOU GUYS ...
...ARE INCREDIBLE.
BIKI
BIKI
BIKI
I CAN'T BELIEVE YOU CAN GATHER OUR LIMBS AND REATTACH THEM.

BIKI
SORRY, BUT PLEASE BE QUIET.
I'M NOT AS SKILLED AS CYNTHIA...
...SO IF I LOSE CONCENTRATION, I'LL FAIL.
BIKI
BIKI
BIKI
I WOULDN'T HOLD A GRUDGE EVEN IF YOU DID.
YOU SAVED MY *LIFE*.
BIKI
!
!
CAPTAIN MIRIA.

READ THIS WAY

GA
SHA

!
HEY ...
IS THAT...

GASHA
...
IT'S ...

OOOO

TODAY THE WARRIORS' REVOLT AND THE DEATH OF LIMT ENDED THE LONG HISTORY OF THE ORGANIZATION IN THIS LAND.

クレイモア
Claymore

Scene 127: Claws and Fangs of the Abyss, Part 8

ZU
ZU
SCENE 127: CLAWS AND FANGS OF THE ABYSS, PART 8

ZU
ZU
ZU
ZU
ZU
ZU

I'M SORRY ...
...ABOUT WHAT I DID TO YOU.

IT'S ALL RIGHT.
I UNDERSTAND YOUR POSITION AS NUMBER 10.
EVERYONE KNOWS WHAT YOU DID FOR US LATER.
THE TWINS ARE SURE TO OFFER THANKS FOR SAVING THEIR LIVES.
AT LEAST WE'RE BOTH ALIVE.
...
SOB
SOB

READ THIS WAY

I'M SHOCKED.
!
THAT LITTLE BRAT IS STILL ALIVE...
...AND GREW UP TO BE THIS BIG.

I REC-OGNIZED *YOU* AT A GLANCE.
TIME PASSES, BUT WARRIORS LOOK THE SAME.

I'M LOOKING FOR CLARE.
DO YOU HAVE ANY INFOR-MATION ABOUT HER?

WE'VE GOT MORE THAN INFO.
TAP
TAP
TAP
UNTIL RECENTLY, WE'VE BEEN WITH HER THESE SEVEN YEARS.

!
THEN CLARE IS...

YES, SHE'S ALIVE.
!
BUT SHE'S IN A DIFFICULT SITUATION.

DIFFICULT...
...SITUATION?

IT'S A LONG STORY...
...THAT SPANS OUR ASSIGNMENT UP NORTH TO THE PRESENT.

CLARE SPENT SEVEN YEARS LOOKING FOR YOU...
...AND RISKED HER LIFE FOR VENGEANCE.

!

READ THIS WAY

WHAT IS IT?

IS SOME-THING WRONG?

I DON'T LIKE IT...
THIS COULD BE A VERY BAD DEVELOP-MENT.

!

THE REMAIN-ING ABYSSAL ONE...
...SAID THE SAME THING AS THE RESIDUAL WILL OF CLARE'S OBJECT OF REVENGE.

!
WHAT ?

WHAT...
...DO YOU MEAN?

READ THIS WAY

I DIDN'T HEAR IT CLEARLY...
...BUT HER MOUTH MOVED THE SAME WAY.
I DON'T KNOW HOW, BUT THE THREE REVIVED ABYSSAL ONES ARE RELATED TO CLARE'S OPPONENT.

AND INSTEAD OF JUST IGNORING US AND LEAVING...
...THE REMAINING ONE...
...APPEARED TO BE PULLED BY SOME KIND OF FORCE.

HUH?
PULLED BY SOME-THING?
BUT TO WHERE?
!
THAT'S IT...
DAMN IT!

SHE WAS HEADED TOWARD WHERE THE SUN SETS...
IN HER PATH LIE LAUTREC, IN THE WESTERN LANDS, AND THE HOLY CITY OF RABONA IN THE CENTRAL LANDS OF TOULOUSE.

WHAT ...

!

IF SOME KIND OF POWER, INCLUDING CLARE, IS KEEPING HER OPPONENT SEALED...
...THEN WHAT COULD BREAK THE SEAL IS HER OWN POWER FROM THE OUTSIDE.

IT'S GOING TO UNLEASH ON THE HOLY CITY OF RABONA...
...A POWER YOU SAY IS GREATER THAN AN ABYSSAL ONE'S.

READ
THIS
WAY

GA
DAMN IT!
K

I CAN'T BE-LIEVE ...
...I CARRIED THAT THING THERE!

IT ISN'T ALL YOUR FAULT.
EVERYONE, INCLUDING MYSELF, TOOK IT THERE.

...

WE'VE GOT TO STOP HER.
WE'VE GOT TO DEFEAT THAT ABYSSAL ONE...
...BEFORE IT REACHES RABONA...

BUT THEN ...
...WHAT ABOUT CLARE?

!!

IF WE LEAVE THE SEAL IN PLACE, WE'LL NEVER GET CLARE OUT.
BESIDES, WE'RE TALKING ABOUT AN ABYSSAL ONE. COULD ALL OF US TOGETHER EVEN BEAT HER?

SHE KILLED HYSTERIA ...
...AND DEFEATED AND ATE THE OTHER ONE.
SHE IS THE STRONGEST OF THE THREE.
...
URGH ...
THEN...
...WHAT DO YOU SUGGEST?

READ THIS WAY

NOTHING DIFFICULT.
IT'S QUITE SIMPLE.

IF WE CAN'T STOP HER...
...THEN WE GET CLARE OUT ON OUR OWN BEFORE-HAND.

WHAT?

...

B...
BUT ...
...IF WE DO THAT...

WE DON'T KNOW HOW THE ABYSSAL ONE HEADED FOR RABONA WILL UNDO THE SEAL...
...BUT THE WORST CASE WOULD BE THOSE TWO SYNCHRONIZING AND *FORCING* IT OPEN.
THEN CLARE'S OPPONENT WOULD BE EVEN STRONGER.

SO WE SHOULD UNDO THE SEAL FIRST...
...AND LOOSE A DISTINCT INDIVIDUAL AT THE ABYSSAL ONE.
IF IT GOES WELL, THE ABYSSAL ONE WILL REGAIN ITS SENSES.
THEN IF THEY SQUARE OFF, THERE'S A SMALL CHANCE THAT AN OPPORTUNITY MAY ARISE.

READ THIS WAY

THAT'S ASKING A LOT.
DO YOU REALLY THINK THAT WILL HAPPEN?

I DON'T KNOW.
IT DOES SOUND LIKE A MIRACLE.
BUT AT THE MOMENT...
...A MIRACLE DOESN'T SEEM ENTIRELY IMPLAUSIBLE.

WHEN CLARE WAS SEARCHING FOR THE BOY UP NORTH...
...I THOUGHT IT WAS A WASTE OF TIME.

THERE WAS NO WAY SHORT OF A MIRACLE ...
...THAT A BOY SOLD INTO SLAVERY...
...COULD SURVIVE THOSE WAR-TORN LANDS.

BUT THAT BOY IS HERE WITH US NOW.
IF CLARE HADN'T HAD FAITH...
...WE MIGHT STILL BE UP NORTH, NEVER HAVING FOUND HIM.

SO HERE'S WHAT I THINK...
MIRACLES AREN'T SOMETHING YOU WISH FOR. YOU SEIZE THEM USING YOUR OWN STRENGTH!

HMPH.

READ THIS WAY

SO WHAT DO WE DO?
TMP
EVEN AT TOP SPEED, I'M NOT SURE WE COULD REACH RABONA FIRST.

WE COULD OVERTAKE THE ABYSSAL ONE...
...BUT I WOULD PREFER TO STAY FAR ENOUGH AWAY THAT SHE DOESN'T SENSE OUR YOMA ENERGY.
WELL, *I'VE* GOT AN IDEA.
!

I CAME HERE BY SHIP.
IF WE FOLLOW THE SOUTHERN COASTLINE, CUT PAST THE PENINSULA, AND CROSS THE GULF, WE'LL REACH THE CENTRAL LANDS.
!
BY... SHIP?

READ THIS WAY

IT WOULD ONLY TAKE HALF THE TIME.
I BET THAT'S HOW THOSE GUYS IN BLACK GOT AROUND.
BY USING HIDDEN SHIPS AND PORTS.

I SEE...
...WHAT YOU MEAN.
ALL RIGHT, LET'S DO IT.
THAT WAY WE SHOULD GET THERE IN PLENTY OF TIME.

SORRY, BUT YOU'RE COMING WITH US.
IT'LL BE DANGER-OUS...
...BUT YOUR VOICE MIGHT REACH CLARE BETTER THAN OURS.
IF IT MEANS SEEING CLARE ...
...I'D GO WHETHER OR NOT YOU INVITED ME.

MIS-TER...
!
...ARE YOU GOING SOME-WHERE?
HEY NOW, GUYS...
ZA
YOU'RE FREE NOW...
...SO DON'T LOOK SO DOWN!
WITH ALL THESE NEW SISTERS...
...YOU'LL BE FINE WITHOUT ME.
Pat
Pat
THEY LIKE HIM.
I GUESS THAT'S BECAUSE HE SAVED THEM.
...

READ
THIS
WAY

HEY...
IT WOULD BE GREAT IF THAT GUY...
...REALLY COULD DRAW OUT CLARE...

...BUT THERE'S A HIGH POSSIBILITY SHE'LL COME OUT RAW.
WHAT ABOUT THAT?

!

!!

SHE COULD COME OUT LIKE SHE WAS BEFORE TREATMENT.
THEN WE WOULD HAVE TO DO IT RIGHT THEN AND THERE.

IF THAT BOY SEES IT...
WELL, CLARE WOULDN'T WANT HIM TO SEE THAT...
I MEAN...

ZA
!

ZA
H...
ZA
ZA
HEY ... ...DE-NEVE?

ZA
!

GU

BW

SH

TAKE A GOOD LOOK.
THIS IS WHAT OUR BODIES ARE LIKE.

!
WH-WHOA...

DENEVE!
WHAT ARE YOU...

WE WARRIORS...
...AND EVEN THOSE TRAINEES YOU HELPED...
...ARE ALL LIKE THIS.

AND THAT INCLUDES...
...YOUR DEAR CLARE.

!!

READ THIS WAY

IT IS LIKELY THAT IF CLARE COMES OUT IN RABONA...
...SHE WILL LOOK THIS WAY, OR SIMILAR.

BY "SIMILAR," I MEAN WITHOUT BEING TREATED.
WHICH MEANS WE WOULD HAVE TO DO IT.
AFTER, SHE WILL LOOK LIKE THIS.

REMEM-BER THIS WELL.
THIS IS WHAT WE'RE LIKE. IT'S WHAT CLARE'S BODY IS LIKE.
IF YOU SEE CLARE...
...AND CAN ACCEPT HER CONDITION...

... THEN YOU MUST ...

...NOT HESITATE TO HOLD HER TO YOU.

READ THIS WAY

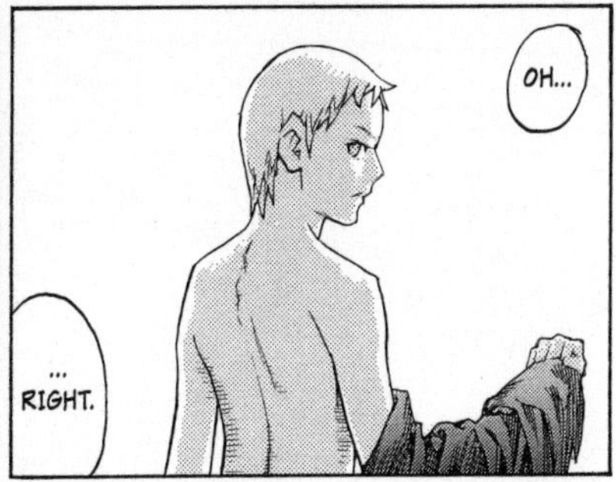
OH...
...RIGHT.

goso
goso
goso

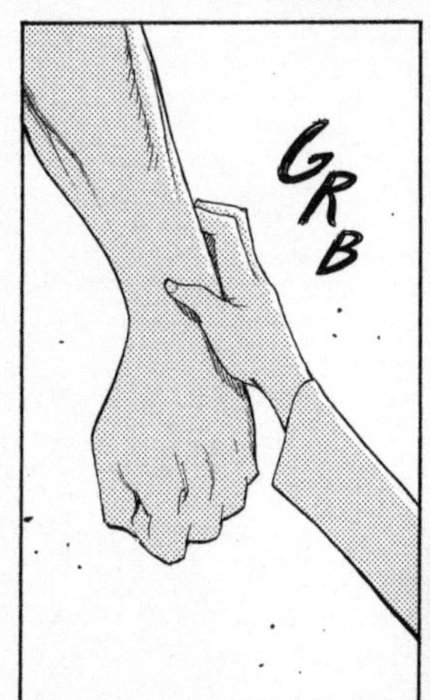
GRB

M-MISTER...
...WE...
...UM...

GASHI
!!
!

SORRY. I ACTED LIKE I WAS NEVER COMING BACK.
BUT I WILL, WHEN ALL THIS IS OVER...
...AND WE'LL HAVE A GOOD TIME.

MISTER...
SNIFF
SNIFF
SOB...
SOB...

YOU'VE GOT TO.
SOB
SOB
OKAY.
WAAAH...
WE'LL BE WAITING...
YOU GOTTA PROMISE...
YEAH, I PROMISE.

READ THIS WAY

HMPH.

HE HAD ME SCARED FOR A MOMENT.

ZA

TABITHA ...

I WANTED YOU TWO...

...TO STAY AND HEAL THE WARRIORS, BUT...

ZA

I KNEW YOU'D SAY THAT...
...SO I ALREADY DID EVERY-THING I COULD.
ONE OF THE WARRIORS HAD AN INSTINCT FOR IT...
...AND WITH A LITTLE INSTRUCTION SOON SURPASSED ME.
SO I'M DONE HERE.

READ THIS WAY

THIS FATEFUL BOND GOES BACK TO THE WAR-TORN NORTH SEVEN YEARS AGO.
WE ALL WANT TO HELP CLARE.

HEH HEH ...

ALL RIGHT ...

WE GO TOGETHER.
WE SET OUT AT SUNRISE TOMORROW ...
...FOR THE HOLY CITY OF RABONA.

クレイモア
Claymore

Scene 128: Mark of the Warrior, Part 1

Scene 128: Mark of the Warrior, Part 1

WOW. WE MADE IT FROM THE ORGANIZATION'S HEADQUARTERS TO RABONA IN TEN DAYS.
IT WOULD HAVE TAKEN US TWENTY ON FOOT.
SHIPS ARE MUCH FASTER.

THAT'S BECAUSE ...
...THEY DON'T HAVE TO GO UP AND DOWN MOUNTAINS OR WIND THROUGH FORESTS.
WE ALSO CAUGHT THE OCEAN CURRENT.

TA-BITHA.
YES?
THE ABYSSAL ONE'S YOMA ENERGY IS STILL FAR AWAY.
IT ISN'T MOVING PARTICULARLY FAST.
WE'RE SIX OR SEVEN DAYS AHEAD OF IT.

READ THIS WAY

THEN WE SHOULD HAVE...
...ENOUGH TIME.

IT'S BEEN SO LONG.
I HOPE SID AND GALK ARE DOING WELL.

ZA
!

!
OH...
...HELLO.

HM?
DO YOU LIVE IN RABONA?
NO.
I CAME FROM FURTHER WEST.

IF YOU'RE GOING TO RABONA, WANNA GO TOGETHER?
WE'RE GOING THERE OUR-SELVES.

NO, I'LL STAY HERE.
BESIDES, NO RESIDENTS ARE LEFT IN THE HOLY CITY ANYWAY.
smile

HUH?!
NONE?
WHY NOT?

GASHI
THEY DON'T APPEAR THREATEN-ING...
...BUT DON'T GO ANY CLOSER.

READ THIS WAY

!!

WHAT'S GOING ON?
IF YOU LOOK CLOSELY ...
...THEY'RE SURROUND-ING RABONA.

!
BA

THEY'RE ALL...
... AWAKENED BEINGS.

!
AWAK-ENED...
... BEINGS?

YOU MUST HAVE SEEN IT WITH CLARE.
THEY WERE IN THE ORGANI-ZATION TOO.
THEY'RE THE MONSTERS THAT RESULT WHEN WARRIORS LOSE CONTROL.

!!

THEY'RE ALL FAIRLY STRONG.
THEY MUST HAVE BEEN SINGLE DIGITS.
AND THEY ALL POSSESS HIGHER-CLASS STRENGTH.

READ THIS WAY

YOU SAID NO RESIDENTS ARE IN THE HOLY CITY.
WHAT DID YOU DO?

WE DIDN'T DO ANYTHING.
THEY LEFT A FEW DAYS AGO, LEAVING ONLY A FEW SOLDIERS BEHIND.

THEY ...
...LEFT?

YOU SHOULD ASK THE SOLDIERS ABOUT IT.
SOME OF YOUR KIND ARE THERE, TOO.

!

YES ...
GALATEA, CLARICE AND MIATA.
I CAN SENSE THEIR YOMA ENERGY IN THE HOLY CITY.

TCH!

SO WHAT'RE *YOU* GUYS...
...DOING HERE AT A TIME LIKE THIS?

WE'RE JUST...
!
...CURIOUS.

IT SURPASSES US, AND EVEN AN ABYSSAL ONE.
IT IS THE GREATEST POWER IN THE HISTORY OF WARRIORS.
WE'RE SURROUNDING IT, BUT WE ALSO JUST WANT TO SEE IT.

READ THIS WAY

AND WE WANTED TO SEE THE FACES OF THOSE WHO DEFEATED THE ORGANIZATION...

...WHICH HAD RULED THIS LAND FOR SO MANY YEARS.

!

WHY?

WE AREN'T FOOLS.
SINCE THE TENSE RELATIONSHIP BETWEEN ABYSSAL ONES BROKE DOWN AND THE ORGANIZATION MADE ITS MOVE...
...WE TEND TO GET DETAILED INFORMATION ON WHAT INFLUENCES WHETHER WE LIVE OR DIE.

WE NEVER DREAMED...
...THE ORGANIZATION WOULD DISAPPEAR.

SO THERE YOU HAVE IT.
WE ALL JUST CHOSE TO VISIT THIS EXTREME PLACE.
EVERYONE BELIEVES THAT IF WORST COMES TO WORST, WE CAN ESCAPE ON OUR OWN.

WE'RE A GALLERY OF ROGUES ...
...HOPING TO LAY EYES ON AN INTERESTING SIGHT.

LET'S GO.
ZA
!

READ THIS WAY

H-HEY...
...IS IT ALL RIGHT TO LET THEM GO?

HIS NAME IS CHRONOS. THE MAN BEHIND HIM IS LARS.
THEY WERE NUMBERS 4 AND 6 IN THE TIME OF MALE WARRIORS.

!

THE GIRL WHO FIRST SPOKE IS A FORMER NUMBER 2 CALLED OCTAVIA THE WILD HORSE.
THERE'S ALSO A FORMER NUMBER 5 AND 3.
TOGETHER THEY COULD BE STRONGER THAN THE APPROACHING ABYSSAL ONE.

BUT THEY'RE NOT LYING ABOUT BEING CURIOUS.
AS WARRIORS WITH EXPERIENCE IN BATTLE, IT'S NO SURPRISE THEY WANT TO SEE THE STRONGEST WARRIOR IN HISTORY AS AN AWAKENED BEING.

BUT IF THE WORST COMES TO PASS ...
...WHETHER THEY CAN REALLY ESCAPE UNHARMED...
...IS ANOTHER STORY.

!!!
TMP
TMP
CAPTAIN MIRIAAA!

EVEN *YOU* CALL HER CAPTAIN NOW?
WHY ARE YOU HERE?
WHAT'S HAPPEN-ING OUT THERE?!

CALM DOWN, CLARICE.
WE'RE THE ONES WITH QUESTIONS.
SOB
SOB
SOB

READ
THIS
WAY

ZA
I'M SUR-PRISED.

I NEVER THOUGHT ...
...YOU WOULD COME BACK ALIVE.

GALA-TEA.

I'M SORRY THAT MY ACTIONS ...
... RESULTED IN AWAKENED BEINGS ATTACKING THE CITY.

THAT'S IN THE PAST.
THE SITUATION IS WORSE NOW.

WE HEARD FROM THOSE OUT-SIDE.
THE RESIDENTS HAVE LEFT THE CITY.
WHAT HAPPENED?

INSTEAD OF EXPLAINING...
...IT WOULD BE FASTER TO SHOW YOU.

HEY!
ARE YOU STILL ALIVE...
...YOU SNOT-NOSED BRAT?
!

SID!
GALK!

LONG TIME NO SEE!
IT'S GOOD TO SEE YOU AGAIN.

YOU'VE GROWN SOME MORE.
SOON YOU'LL BE AS TALL AS GALK.

THIS WAY.
ZA
FOLLOW ME.
!

READ
THIS
WAY

WHAT ABOUT THE REMAINING SOLDIERS?
THEY'RE VOLUNTEERS.
I SAID WE WOULD BE FINE, BUT THEY WANT TO DEFEND THEIR OWN CITY.

THEY ARE PREPARED TO DIE.
WE CAN SAY NOTHING ABOUT IT.
HERE WE ARE.
ZA
!
THIS IS IT.

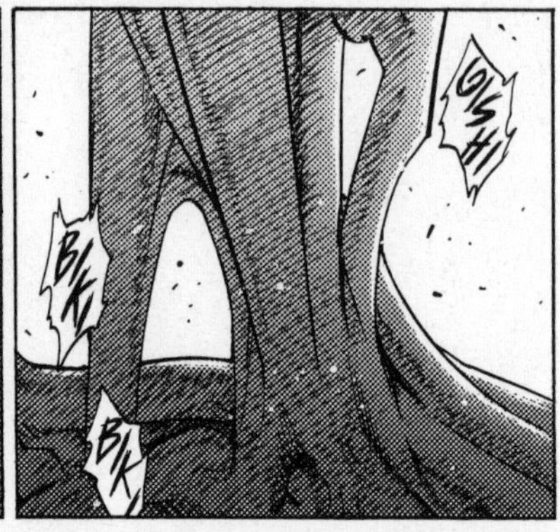
GISHI
BIKI
BIKI

BIKI
BIKI
GISHI

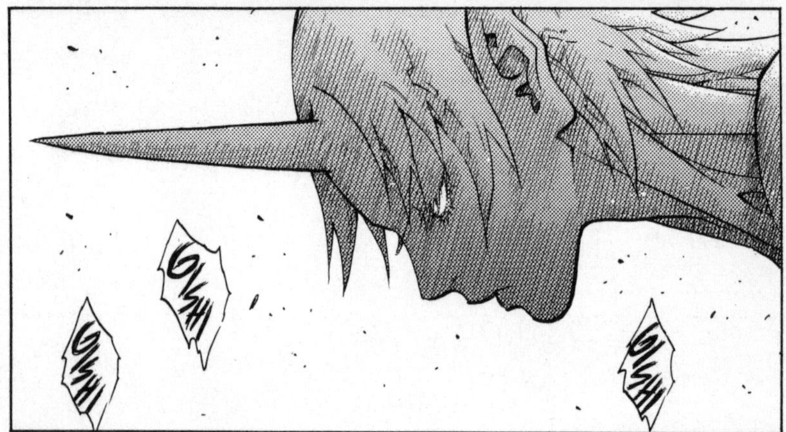
GISHI
GISHI
GISHI

W... WHAT...
...IS THIS?

NO WAY...
SHAK
!

YOU GOTTA BE KIDDING!
SHE'S ...
...HALF-WAY OUT!

READ
THIS
WAY

!!

DE-
NEVE
...
IS
THIS
HER?
IS
THIS
THE
ONE
WHO
...

YEAH.
I NEVER
WANTED
TO SEE
HER FACE
AGAIN.
SHE'S
DEFINITELY
THE ONE
WHO'S
STRONGER
THAN AN
ABYSSAL ONE.

AS
YOU
CAN
SEE...
...THE MASS
BEGAN
CHANGING
TEN DAYS AGO,
AND BY FIVE
DAYS AGO
HAD CLEARLY
TAKEN A
HUMANOID
FORM.

...
...
WHA
...

WE THOUGHT ABOUT STABBING OR MOVING HER BEFORE SHE GETS OUT...
...BUT WE HAD NO IDEA WHAT EFFECT SUCH STIMULATION MIGHT HAVE, SO WE LET HER BE.

SO THAT'S WHY YOU HAD...
...THE RESIDENTS EVACUATE.
IT WAS THE RIGHT CHOICE.
THE WRONG STIMULATION...
...COULD HAVE HASTENED THE APPROACHING ABYSSAL ONE.

APPROACHING...
...ABYSSAL ONE?

GALATEA, I HAVE SOMETHING TO TELL YOU...
...AND ALL OF THE REMAINING SOLDIERS.

READ THIS WAY

I WANTED TO TELL THE PRIESTS AS WELL...
...BUT PERHAPS IT'S JUST AS WELL THAT THEY EVACUATED WITH THE RESIDENTS.

IT...
...DOESN'T SOUND LIKE I'M GOING TO LIKE WHAT I HEAR.

SORRY ...
...BUT YOU'RE RIGHT.

THE HOLY CITY OF RABONA ...
...COULD BE GONE IN JUST A FEW DAYS.

READ THIS WAY

TCH!
SKRTCH
SKRTCH

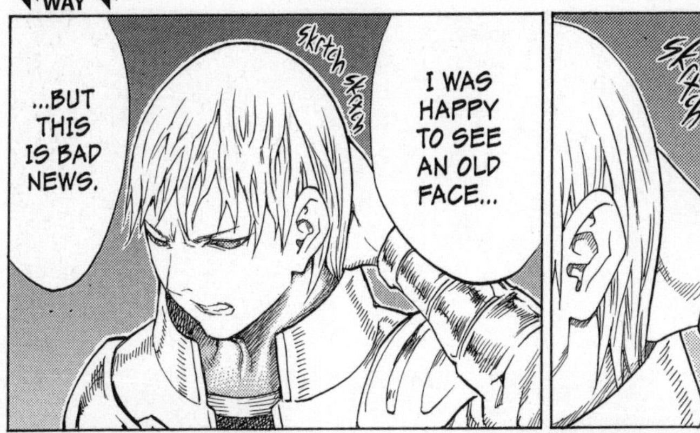
SKRTCH SKRTCH
I WAS HAPPY TO SEE AN OLD FACE...
...BUT THIS IS BAD NEWS.

I'M SORRY.
WE WILL DO EVERY-THING WE CAN...
...BUT IT'S UNLIKELY THIS WILL GO WELL.

LUCKILY, WE HAVE SOME TIME.
I WANT THE SOLDIERS TO FOLLOW THE RESIDENTS AND LEAVE THE CITY.

SORRY, BUT...
...WE DISCUSSED THAT FIVE DAYS AGO WITH SISTER LATEA.

AND WE DECIDED TO STAY.
THE SITUATION MAY CHANGE...
...BUT OUR DETER-MINATION WON'T.

READ THIS WAY

UNDER-STOOD.
I'M SORRY ...
...I BROUGHT IT UP AGAIN.

UM...
...WHAT ABOUT MIATA AND ME?

OH, RIGHT.

WE WILL TAKE OVER HELPING AS GALATEA'S EYES.
YOU SHOULD BOTH JOIN THE RESIDENTS.

HUH ...?
OH ...

...

B-BUT ...
...IF POSSIBLE ...
...MAY I STAY HERE AS WELL?

HUNH?

!

B-BUT THE PEOPLE HERE...
...HAVE BEEN SO KIND TO ME.
I LOVE THIS PLACE.

WHAT ?!
EEK.
THIS IS A MATTER OF LIFE AND DEATH...
HOW COULD YOU AND YOUR FANCY HAIR POSSIBLY HELP?!

MAMA.
DON'T CRY...
...MAMA...

SO IF I COULD LEND...
...EVEN A LITTLE STRENGTH TO DEFENDING THIS CITY...
...I WANT TO...

I SEE...

READ THIS WAY

FINE. SORRY.
JUST LIKE US...
...YOU ARE A WARRIOR.

CLARICE, MIATA AND THE SOLDIERS WILL DEFEND THE HOLY CITY.
BUT DON'T OVERDO IT. A CITY WITHOUT SURVIVORS ISN'T A CITY.

OKAY!
WE'LL DO OUR BEST.

...
YOU ...
...SHOULD APOLOGIZE LATER.

UNTIL THE MONSTER ARRIVES ...
...USE RABONA HOWEVER YOU WANT.
YOU CAN EAT AND DRINK FOR FREE.

WHEN THE CAPTAIN ASKED ME BEFORE, I WENT ALONE, SO I COULDN'T BRING BACK MUCH...
...BUT THIS TIME A BUNCH OF US WENT TO THE VILLAGE AND RETURNED WITH ALL WE COULD FIND.

AND...
CHAK
!

HUH...
!

IT'S A LITTLE GIFT FROM US.
USE IT OR DON'T, AS YOU LIKE.

READ
THIS
WAY

!

!
!!

CHRONOS ...
YES.

THE ABYS-SAL ONE...
...HAS ACCEL-ERATED HER PACE.

クレイモア

Claymore

Scene 129: Mark of the Warrior, Part 2

GASHA
SCENE 129: MARK OF THE WARRIOR, PART 2

READ THIS WAY
AH...
...AH HA HA HA HA!
WHAT THE HELL?
THIS BRINGS BACK SO MANY MEMORIES IT'S SCARY...
GASHA

IT WAS IN PIETA, UP NORTH.
SEEING HOW GLAD YOU ARE MAKES HAULING IT BACK HERE WORTH IT.

COME TO THINK OF IT, ALL OUR GEAR WAS THERE ...
...IN PREPARATION FOR THE BIG WAR.

YEAH, THERE WAS ENOUGH FOR ALL THOSE WARRIORS.
WE DIDN'T KNOW WHOSE WAS WHOSE, SO WE BROUGHT IT ALL.

THERE'S A LOT MORE IN THE HOLY CITY'S STORAGE.
YOU WON'T LACK FOR GEAR NOW.

GASHA
ALL READY?
WE'LL HEAD OUT SOON.

GO TO HER.

HELP HER.

YOU ALREADY SAVED THIS CITY ONCE...
...SO WE'LL FORGIVE YOU EVEN IF IT'S DESTROYED THIS TIME.
A
GASHI

ZA
GASHI
GASHI

PRI
...
...
SCILLA?

!!

HUNH?

WHAT THE HELL?
DO YOU KNOW...
...THIS MONSTER?

READ THIS WAY

NO...
I DON'T, BUT...
...I FEEL LIKE...
...SHE RESEMBLES SOMEONE I KNOW.

TCH!
GIMME A BREAK.
YOU'RE CON-FUSING.

SO NOW WHAT?
DO WE SURROUND IT AND CHANT HER NAME?

I HATE TO DUMP COLD WATER ON YOUR IDEA...
...BUT AS FAR AS I CAN TELL, CLARE'S YOMA ENERGY HAS ALREADY DISPERSED.
IN THIS STATE, IT MAY BE IMPOSSIBLE TO CALL HER BACK.

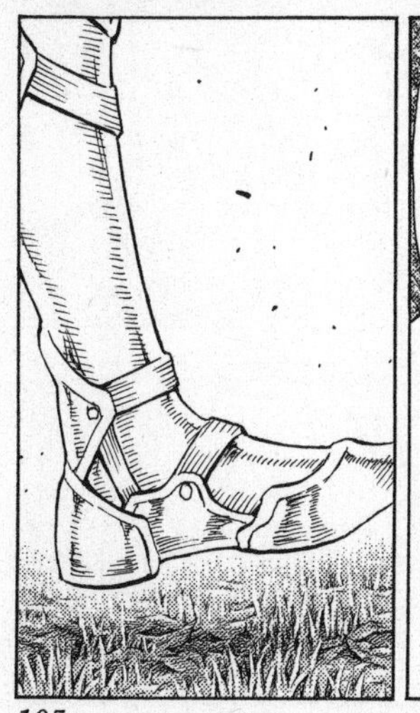

ZA
ZA
!

WAIT!
THAT MASS IS LIKE AN AWAKENED BEING!
IF A HUMAN GOES NEAR...

ZA
!

LET HIM GO.
HE CAME ALL THE WAY FROM THE ORGANI-ZATION FOR THIS.

!

NO ...

HE HAS BEEN...

...SEARCHING FOR CLARE FOR THE LAST SEVEN YEARS.

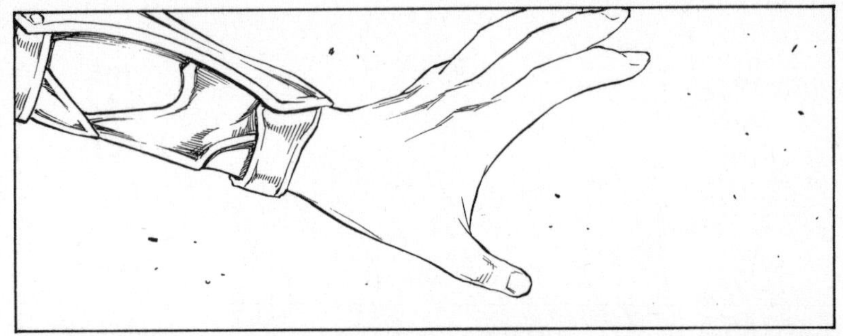

TMP

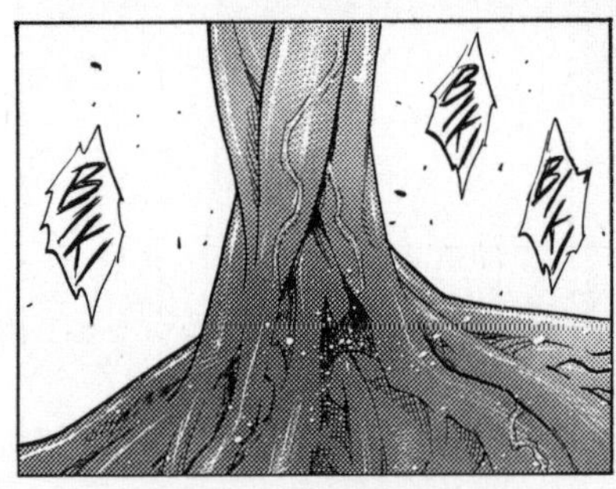

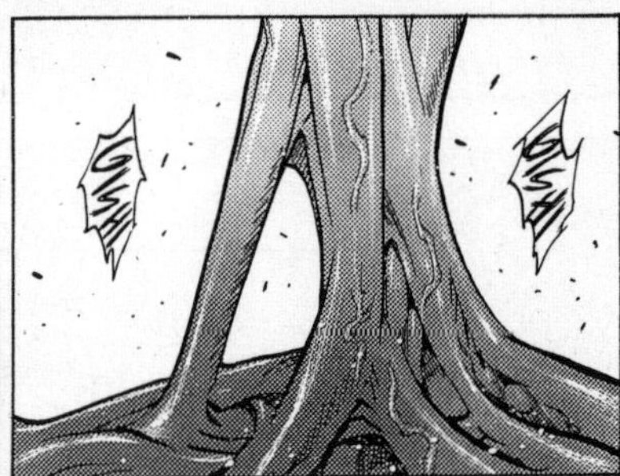

READ THIS WAY

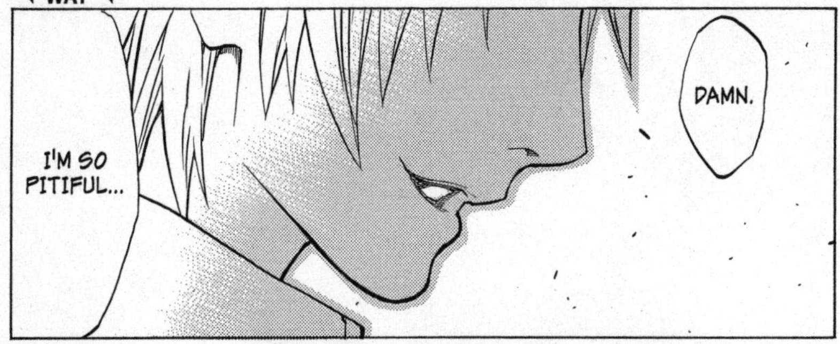
DAMN.
I'M SO PITIFUL...

CAN YOU SEE, CLARE?
MY HANDS ARE TREMBLING.
I FINALLY FIND YOU, AND THIS IS THE STATE I'M IN.

IT'S BEEN SEVEN YEARS ...
...SINCE WE PARTED ON THE MOUNTAIN AND SWORE WE'D MEET AGAIN.
I'VE GROWN UP.
I'M ALMOST AS TALL AS GALK NOW.
I WAS TALLER THAN YOU A LONG TIME AGO.
BIKI

DO
GA
GA

GUH...!
!!
WHAT THE...
STAY BACK!
IT REACTS TO HUMANS!
MIRIA! DENEVE! HELP ME!

READ THIS WAY

GA
DAMN IT!
SHA

I'M FINE!
LEAVE ME BE!
!

HUFF
GSH
HUFF
GSH
GSH
HUFF

IT MISSED MY VITALS.
IT'S JUST INVESTI-GATING MY BODY.

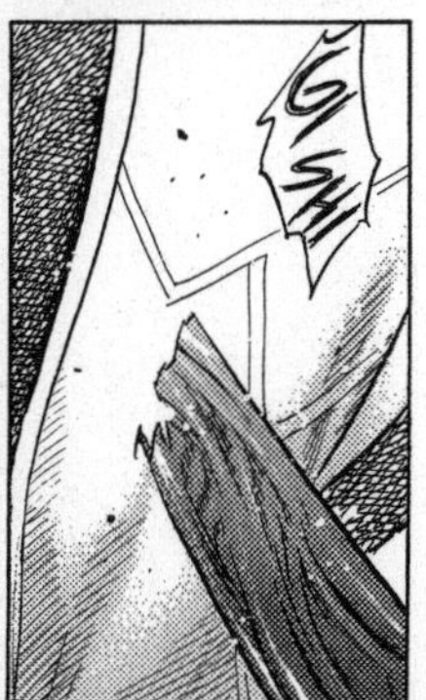
GSH

GSH
GSH

INVESTI-GATING ...?
NO... YOU...

HUFF
HUFF
HUFF
IT'S TRUE...
CLARE IS IN HERE.
HUFF
HUFF
!!
IMPOS-SIBLE...
HOW COULD A HUMAN...
!
BIKI
BIKI
BIKI
BIKI
CLARE IS...
BIKI
BIKI
... BATTLING AS HARD AS SHE CAN...
...TO STOP THE OTHERS FROM BREAKING FREE.
BIKI

CLARE, WHEN YOU WERE SUFFERING IN THE CATHEDRAL ALL I COULD DO WAS CLING TO YOU.

I WAS PITIFUL.

SO I VOWED TO GET STRONGER AND HELP *YOU* NEXT TIME.

I'M...
...GLAD FOR OUR TIME TRAVELING TOGETHER.
I DON'T WANT ANYONE ELSE.
I ONLY WANT TO BE BY YOUR SIDE FOREVER.
!

GOGOM
WHAT THE ...?!

CLA...
CLARE
...

!!
!
TCH!
I KNEW IT! SHE'S UN-TREATED!

UA
A

GOOD. HOLD HER DOWN.
CYNTHIA, BRING THE TOOLS!
UH...
RIGHT.

YUMA, HOLD DOWN HER LOWER HALF...
...OR HER INSIDES WILL SPILL OUT!

READ THIS WAY

HUFF
HUFF
HUFF

EVEN AS CHIL-DREN...
!

...OUR BODIES ARE SPLIT IN HALF LIKE THIS.
YOMA FLESH AND BLOOD IS STUFFED INTO ALL OUR BODY PARTS...
...SO WE BECOME A HALF-YOMA WAR-RIOR.

THE COMPLETED WARRIOR HAS GREATER STRENGTH AND SPEED THAN A YOMA.
THE RESULTS WERE BETTER THAN THE ORGANI-ZATION HAD HOPED.

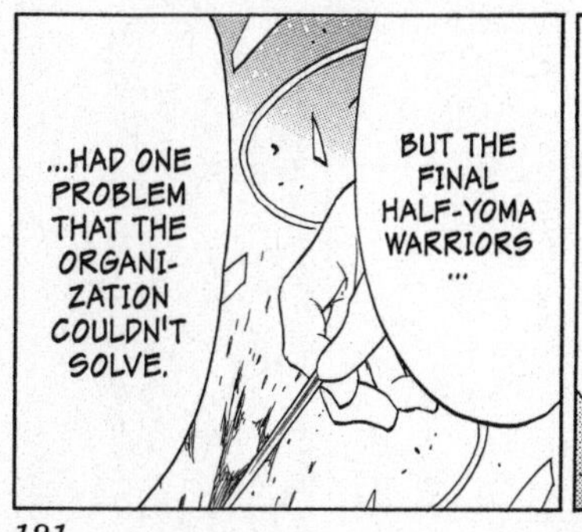
BUT THE FINAL HALF-YOMA WARRIORS ...
...HAD ONE PROBLEM THAT THE ORGANI-ZATION COULDN'T SOLVE.

OUR BODIES ...
...REMAIN SPLIT OPEN.

...

THE ORGANIZATION RESEARCHED AND TESTED, BUT TO NO AVAIL.

ONCE A BODY WAS COMPLETE, THEY COULDN'T CHANGE IT.

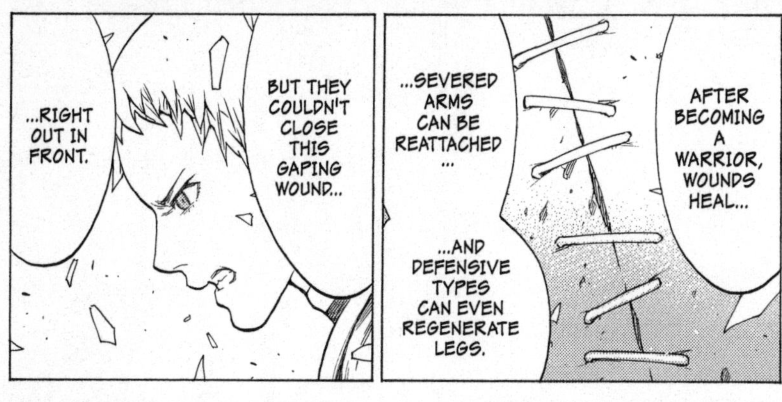

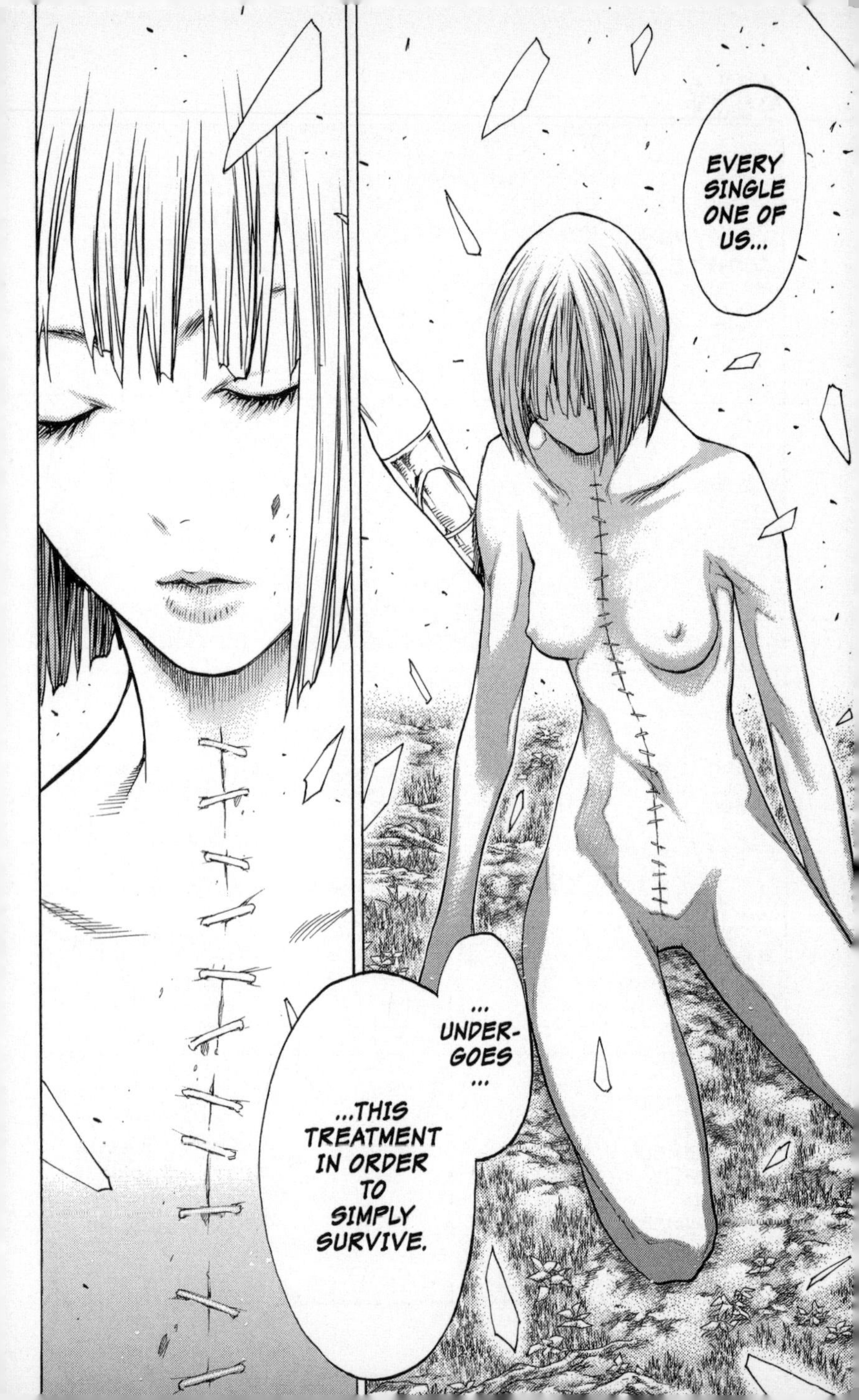
EVERY SINGLE ONE OF US...
... UNDER-GOES ...
...THIS TREATMENT IN ORDER TO SIMPLY SURVIVE.

READ THIS WAY

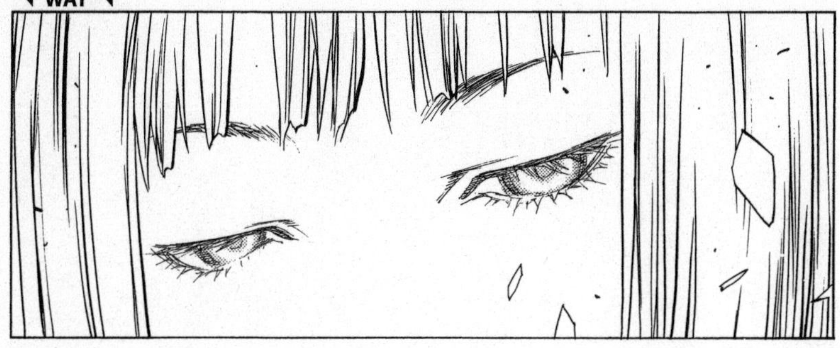

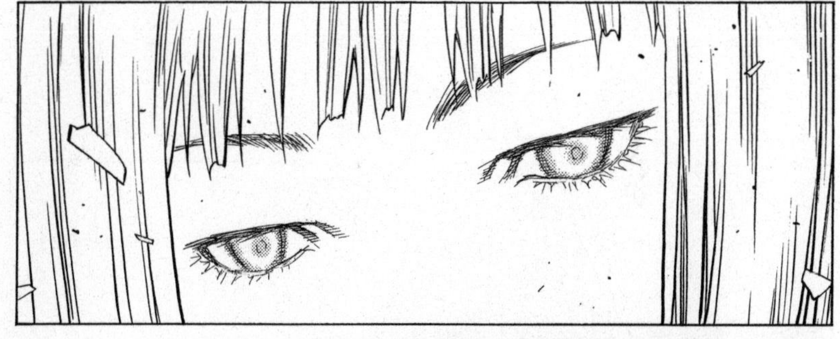

GUYS ...

WHY ...
...AM I...

!

SOB ...
SOB ...
C...
CLARE ...

RAKI ...
IS THAT YOU...?

READ THIS WAY

I'VE WANTED ...

...FOR SO LONG...
...SO VERY LONG...
...TO SEE YOU AGAIN...
... CLARE ...

クレイモア
Claymore

Scene 130: Mark of the Warrior, Part 3

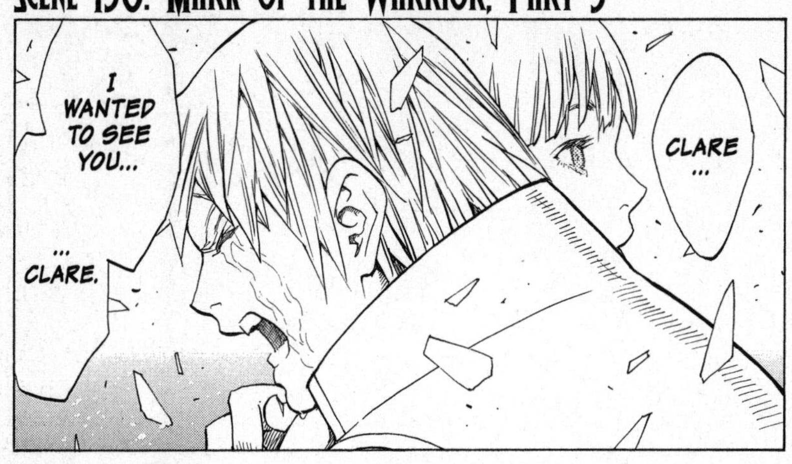

GASHA

ZA

GASHA

GASHA

BIKI
BIKI
BIKI

!

IT'S COMING ...

GO

N

DO
SCENE 130:
MARK OF
THE WARRIOR,
PART 3

WHOA ...

I'M SUR-PRISED.
AFTER THE SEAL BROKE, I THOUGHT IT WOULD KILL EVERYONE THERE...
...OR GO DEVOUR THE PEOPLE IN THE HOLY CITY...

READ THIS WAY

...SO WHY IS IT COMING STRAIGHT HERE...
...TO MEET THOSE OF US ASSEMBLED TO WATCH?

!

THIS...
...IS BAD.
!

LOOK ALIVE...
...LARS.

OO
DO
!
DO BABA
!
!!

GW
DO
GA
GA
GYUA
DO
GA
A

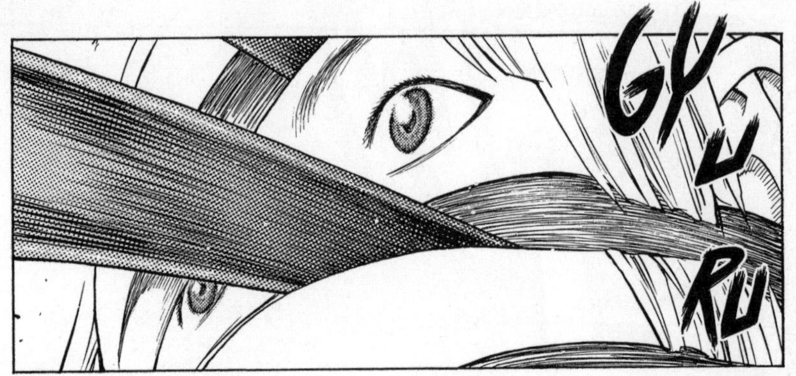

DOGAA

GI SHI
BIKI
BIKI
GISHI
GISHI
GISHI
GISHI
DO
GA
HYUN
HYUN
BIKI

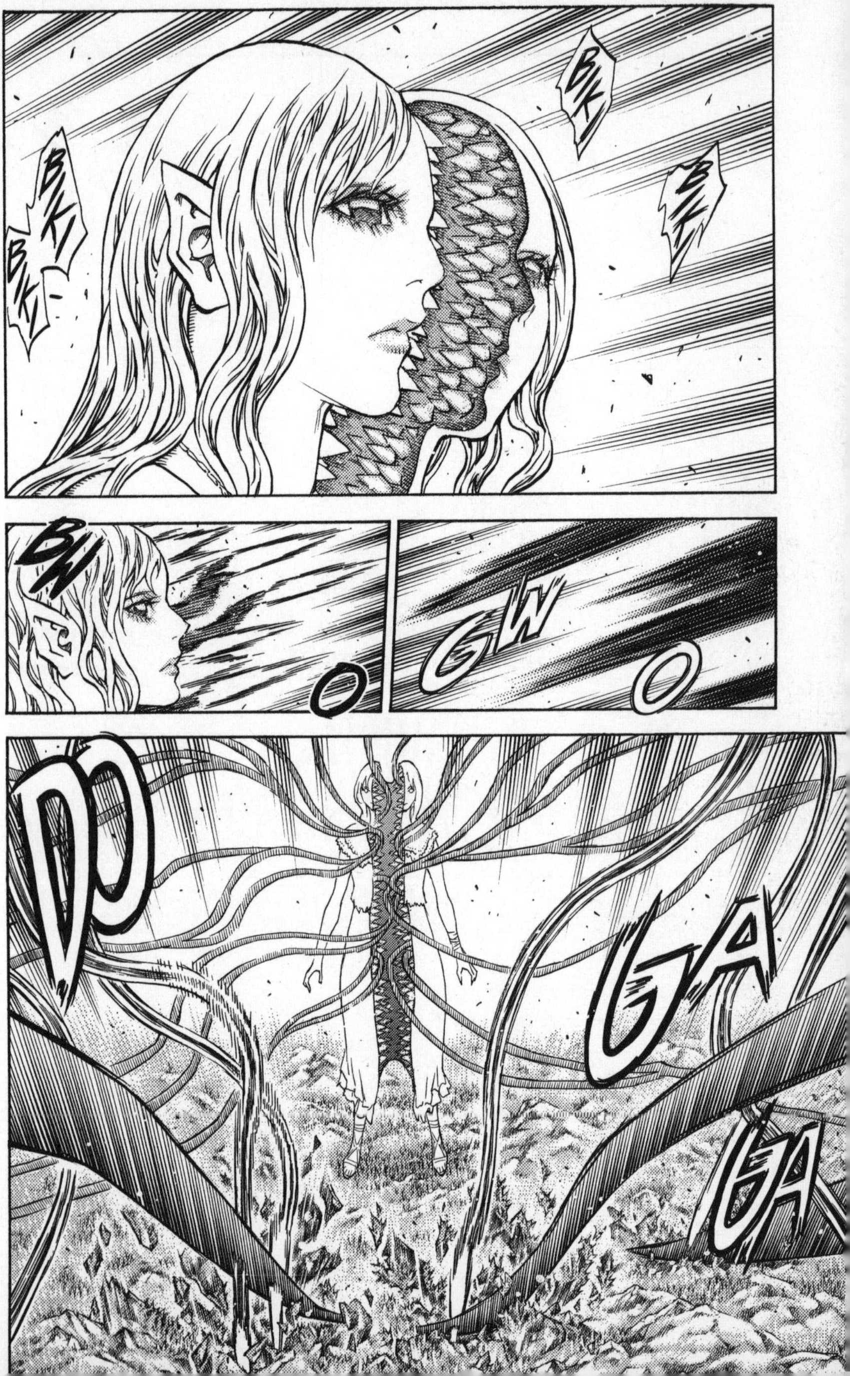

BKI
BKI
BKI
BKI

DO
GA
GA

GUSHI
GA
GA
SHU
GA

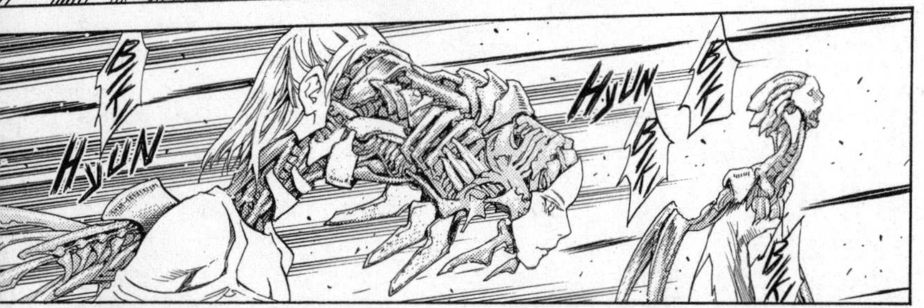
BIKI
BIKI
HYUN
BIKI
BIKI
HYUN

DN
K

!!
UGH!

GUAAGGH!

DOOOO

DOSHA

WHAT THE...

READ THIS WAY

SOME KIND OF BINDING THAT WAS RESTRAINING IT HAS BEEN RELEASED.
NOW IT'S CONTINUING A FIGHT FROM BEFORE.

A...
... FIGHT?

I WAS WRONG. THERE ARE TWO IN THERE.
AND ONE WANTS GREATER STRENGTH...
...SO IT CAME HERE WHERE AWAKENED BEINGS HAVE GATHERED.

!!

PREPARE YOUR-SELF, LARS.
IT'S PUTTING US THROUGH A SIEVE.

I'D SAY ONLY ABOUT HALF OF US...
...WILL MAKE IT THROUGH ALIVE.

WHAT ...
WHAT IS HAPPENING?

I THINK ...
!
...IT'S A BATTLE FOR FLESH AND BLOOD.

ONE IS AN ABSOLUTE MONSTER SURPASS-ING AN ABYSSAL ONE...
...AND THE OTHER IS AN UNCONSCIOUS ORGANISM SEEKING TO EAT ALL LIFE IN THIS LAND.
THE STRONGER ONE WILL TAKE THAT BODY FOR ITS OWN.

READ
THIS
WAY

WHAT
...

WH...
WHICH ONE...
...WOULD WE PREFER TO WIN?

WHICHEVER WINS, ONLY HELL AWAITS.
RIGHT NOW THE UNCONSCIOUS LIFE-FORM ABSORBING POWER FROM AROUND IT HAS THE ADVANTAGE.

BUT IF THE APPROACHING ABYSSAL ONE SYNCHRONIZES WITH THE MONSTER...
...THAT WILL SWIFTLY SETTLE THE MATTER.
GASHA

READ THIS WAY

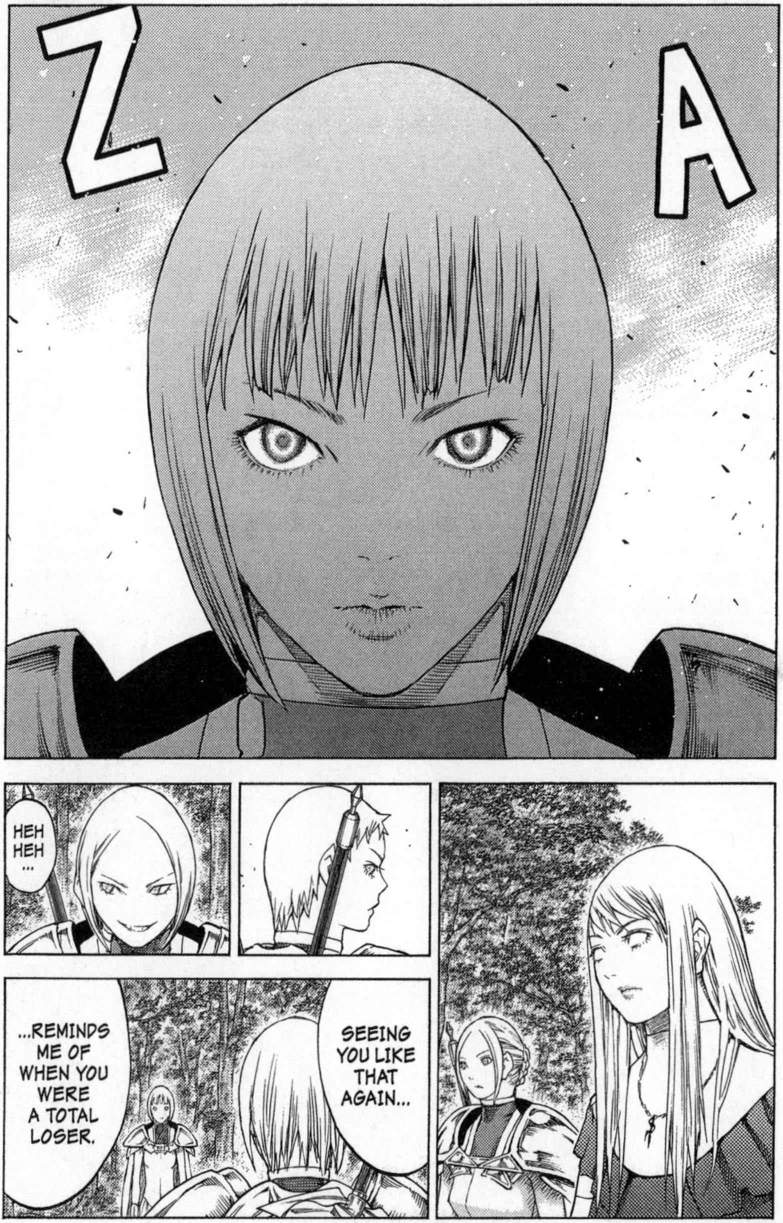

ZA

HEH HEH ...

SEEING YOU LIKE THAT AGAIN...
...REMINDS ME OF WHEN YOU WERE A TOTAL LOSER.

I CAN'T BELIEVE...
...YOU'VE KNOWN ABOUT THAT MONSTER ALL THIS TIME...
...AND CAME ALL THIS WAY WITH A DESIRE FOR REVENGE BURIED INSIDE.

HER NAME IS PRI-SCILLA.
SHE'S THE FORMER NUMBER ONE WHO BEHEADED TERESA.

!

READ
THIS
WAY

I OWE TERESA MY LIFE.
WHEN I WAS A CHILD AND A YOMA DRAGGED ME AROUND AND TORMENTED ME...
...SHE SAVED MY BODY AND SOUL.

TERESA LEFT THE ORGANI-ZATION FOR ME.
THEY PURSUED HER.
SHE THEN FACED PRISCILLA, WHO AWAKENED AS SHE DECAPITATED TERESA.

I TOOK TERESA'S HEAD AND SHOWED UP AT THE GATES OF THE ORGANI-ZATION.
I HAD CHOSEN TO BECOME A WARRIOR.
IN DESPAIR, THAT WAS ALL I COULD DO TO MOVE FORWARD.
AND SO...

...BURIED INSIDE ME IS TERESA'S FLESH.

I AM NOT HALF-YOMA...

...BUT ONE-QUARTER YOMA.

READ THIS WAY

I BECAME A WARRIOR TO GET REVENGE FOR TERESA.
KILLING PRISCILLA IS MY ONLY REASON FOR LIVING.

NO MATTER HOW STRONG SHE IS...
...AND EVEN IF GIVING MY OWN LIFE IS NOT ENOUGH...
...THAT IS AN UNCHANGE-ABLE FACT.

SHING
CLARE.
BASHI
!

AFTER THE BLACK MASS DISAP-PEARED ...
...THAT CLAYMORE WAS STUCK IN THE GROUND.

IT APPEARS TO BE THE SAME ONE THAT WAS SWALLOWED ALONG WITH DENEVE'S RIGHT ARM IN THE WEST.
FATE HAS RETURNED IT TO YOUR HANDS.

TO ONE DEGREE OR ANOTHER ...
...WHETHER THEY LIKE IT OR NOT...
...PEOPLE CHANGE THEIR PATHS IN LIFE THROUGH ENCOUNTERS WITH OTHERS.

ARE YOU TELLING ME THAT ENCOUNTER-ING US, AND OUR TIME TOGETHER...
...MEAN NOTHING IN THE FACE OF YOUR REVENGE?

!

!

GASHA

RIGHT.

IT'S A FATE-FUL BOND...

...FROM THE FIGHT-ING UP NORTH SEVEN YEARS AGO.

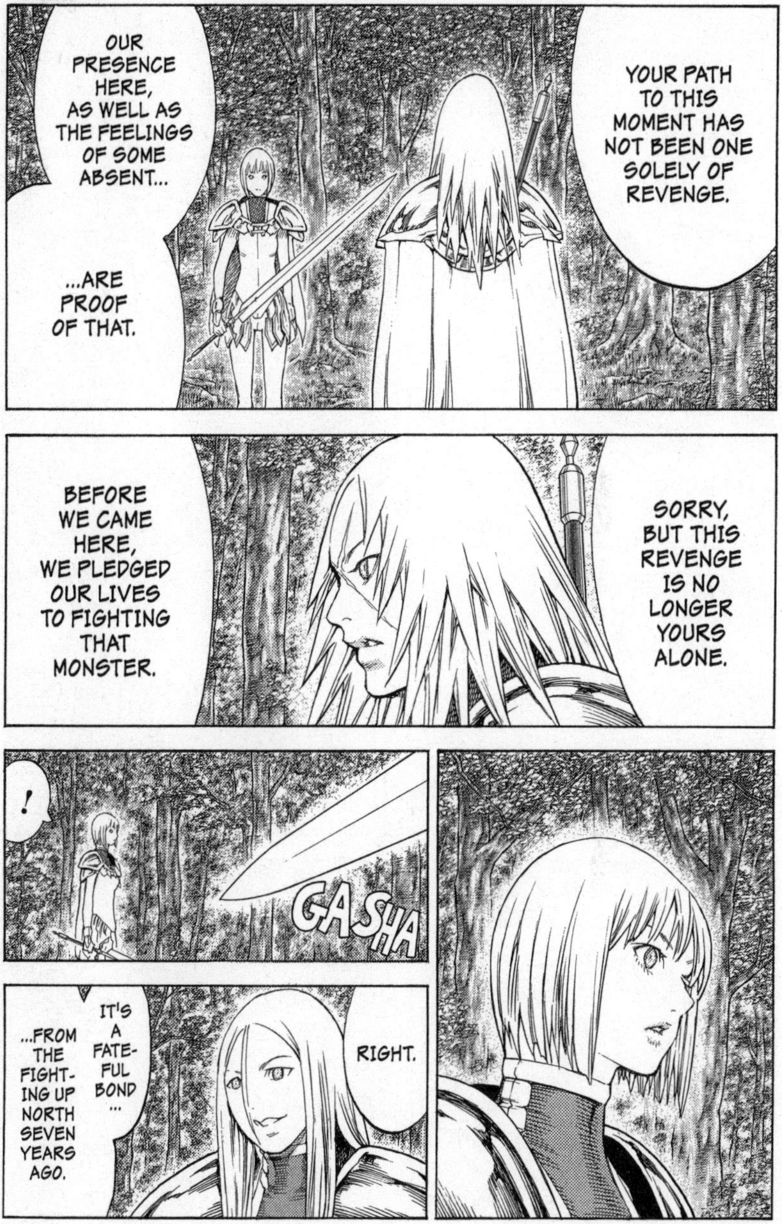

HEH ...

GASHA

YUMA ...
...THAT'S EXACTLY WHAT TABITHA SAID BEFORE WE CAME HERE.

HUH?
OH...
...IT IS?

HMPH.
GASHI

GASHA

WELL ...
...IT'S TRUE.

READ
THIS
WAY

GASHA
HEH
HEH
HEH.

GASHA

GASHA

GASHA

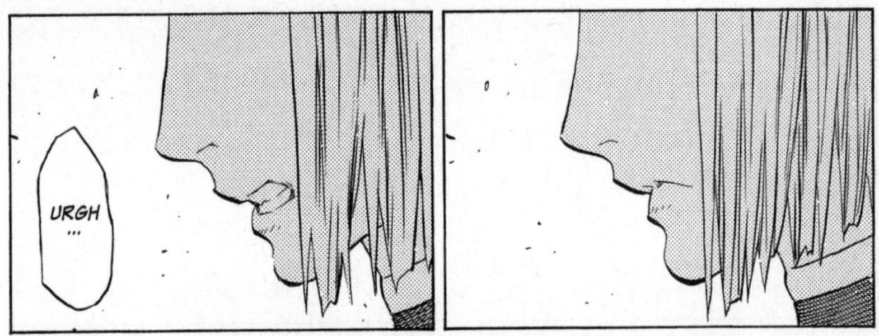
URGH ...

OF COURSE IT MEANS SOME-THING...
YOU ARE ALL...
...ESSENTIAL TO ME AS COMRADES AND FRIENDS!

SO...
...TO-GETHER, LET'S...
...LIVE THROUGH THIS AND SMILE AGAIN!

GA
SHA
Organization Warrior:
129th generation
Former Number 40
Yuma

Organization Warrior:
132nd generation
Former Number 14
Cynthia

Organization Warrior:
141st generation
Former Number 31
Tabitha

Organization Warrior:
135th generation
Former Number 22
Helen

READ
THIS
WAY

Organization Warrior:
135th generation
Former Number 15
Deneve

Organization Warrior:
127th generation
Former Number 6
Miria

Organization Warrior:
150th generation
Former Number 47
Clare

ALL RIGHT, LET'S GO.

AS WARRIORS OF THE ORGANI-ZATION...
...THIS IS OUR LAST UNFINISHED TASK.

クレイモア
Claymore

Scene 131: Mark of the Warrior, Part 4

SCENE 131: MARK OF THE WARRIOR, PART 4

GWO

HYUA
DO
GA
GA
!

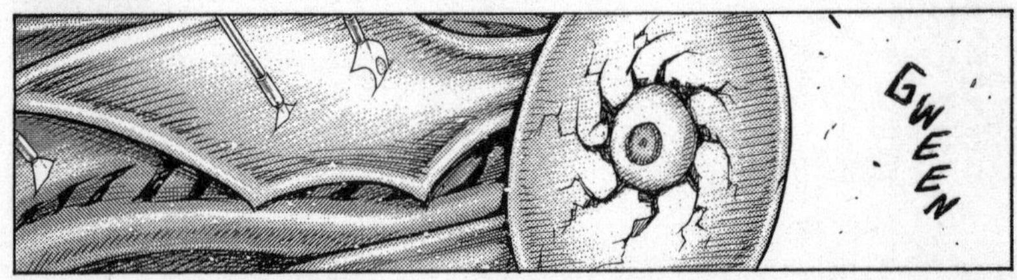
GWEEN

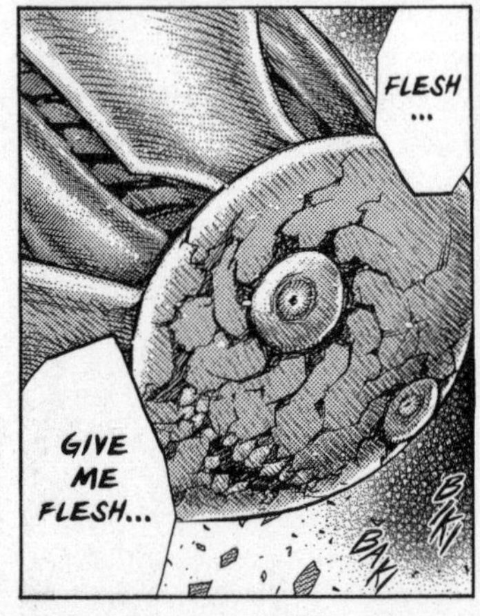
FLESH ...
GIVE ME FLESH...
BAKI
BAKI

DON

!!

FIRE !!

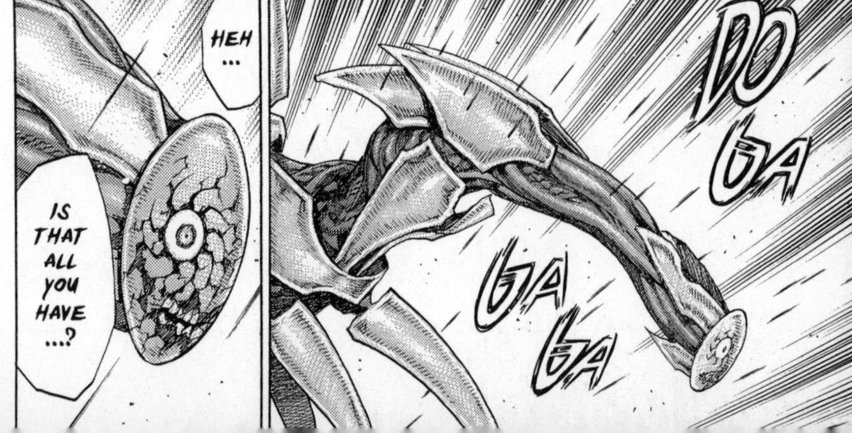

HYU
BYU
PA
GA
SHU
HUP
WHY YOU ...
HRAAH!

!!!
GA
GAH!
MAMA!
GA
SH
!!
YUMA!
CYN-
THIA!
GA
SHA

ZA

!!
HEH HEH ...
THINGS ARE HEATING UP.
DOES THAT MEAN HE AWAKENED THE SLEEPING PRINCESS?
YEAH. PRETTY EASILY.
NOTHING WE DID WORKED, BUT ONE PEEP FROM THAT BRAT AND OUT SHE COMES. IRRITATING, HUH?

HEH HEH HEH!
DON'T BE JEAL-OUS.

IN SOME WAYS, CLARE IS HIS PROTECTOR.
SHE BEARS A STRONG SENSE OF RESPONSI-BILITY FOR HIS LIFE.

BE CARE-FUL.
WITH NOTHING LEFT TO REGRET, SHE MAY TAKE HER LIFE LIGHTLY.

!

GASH
HM?

DO
GA

GA
SHI
ZUSHAAAA
!
URGH!

THANKS.
I OWE YOU ONE.
YOU KNOW...
...DESPITE YOUR APPEARANCE, YOU'RE A GOOD MAN.
!

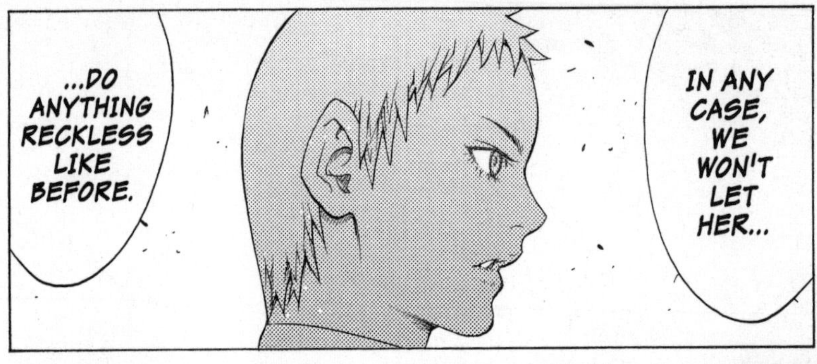
IN ANY CASE, WE WON'T LET HER...
...DO ANYTHING RECKLESS LIKE BEFORE.

GWOO

DOGAAAA
GASHI
GASHI

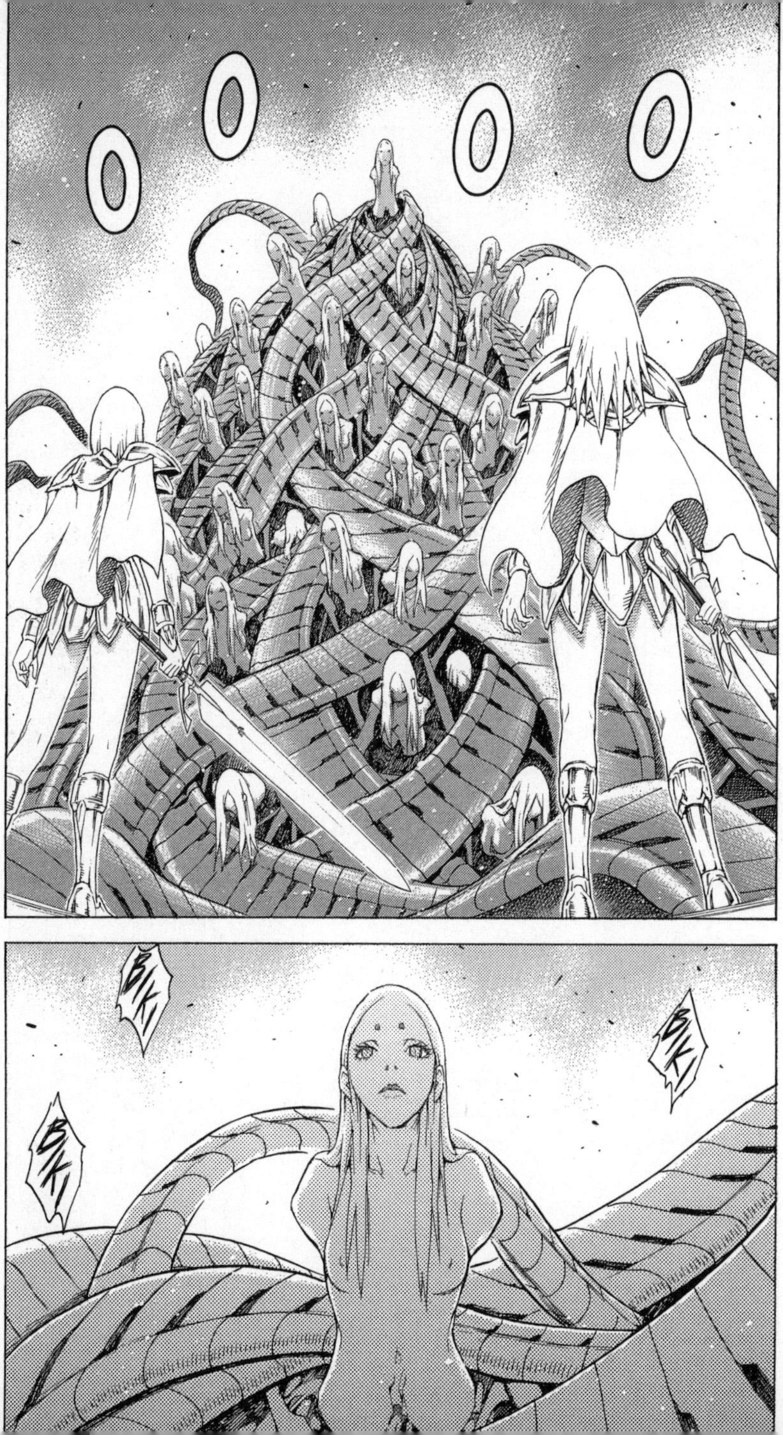

O O O O

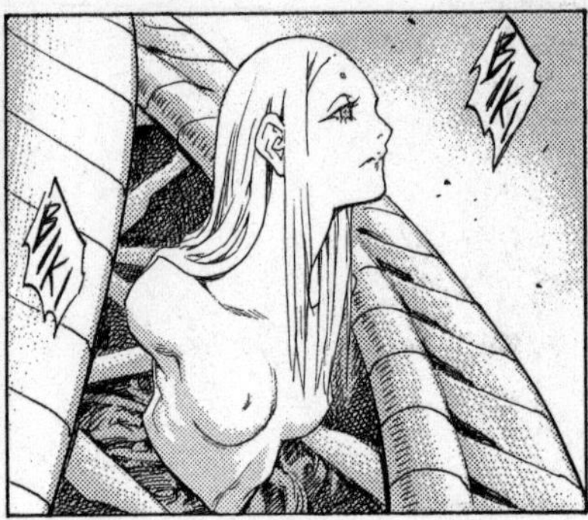
BIKI
BIKI

BIKI
BIKI
BIKI

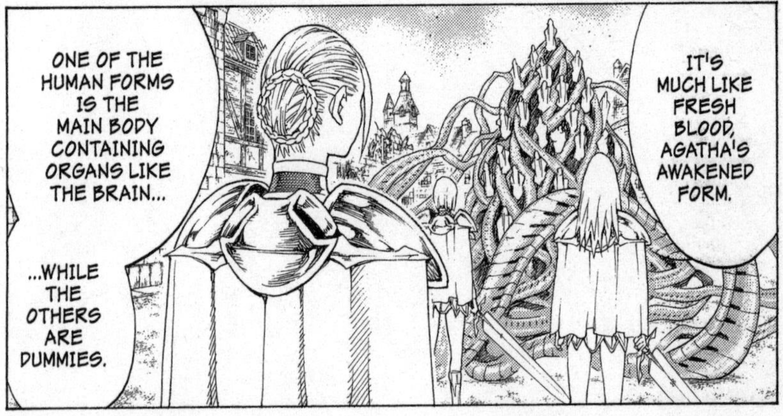
IT'S MUCH LIKE FRESH BLOOD, AGATHA'S AWAKENED FORM.
ONE OF THE HUMAN FORMS IS THE MAIN BODY CONTAINING ORGANS LIKE THE BRAIN...
...WHILE THE OTHERS ARE DUMMIES.

UNLIKE AGATHA, HOWEVER, SHE HAS SKILLFULLY DISTRIBUTED HER YOMA ENERGY TO EACH ONE.
IT IS INCREDIBLY DIFFICULT TO DETERMINE WHICH IS REAL.
HEH...
HEH...
HEH...
HEH...
HEH...
HEH...

READ
THIS
WAY

THAT'S NO...
...BIG DEAL.

!

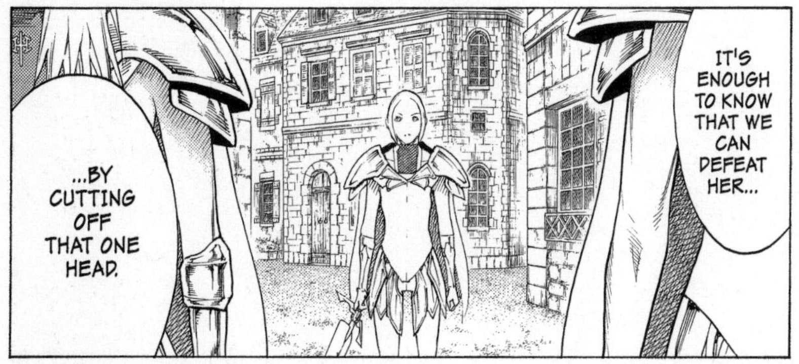
IT'S ENOUGH TO KNOW THAT WE CAN DEFEAT HER...
...BY CUTTING OFF THAT ONE HEAD.

SHE MAY BE AN UPPER-RANKED AWAKENED BEING...
GASHI

... THEN ...

...BUT IF SHE'S SO WEAK THAT PRISCILLA COULD STEAL HER STRENGTH AND THROW HER ALL THE WAY HERE...
GASH

...WE JUST LOP OFF ALL HER HEADS.

GA
SH
GA
GA
GASHU
!!
DO
GA
GA
OOO

HUP
GA
SHU
GA
DO
GA GA
GO
KI
IN

T
MP
DO
GA
SHU
SHA
!
GA
GYU
RU

DO
GA
GA

!!

!

GA
WHAT KIND OF TECH-NIQUE IS THIS?
DO
GA
I'M MOVING DIFFER-ENTLY THAN BEFORE...

READ
THIS
WAY

IT'S LIKE I'VE SURROUNDED MYSELF WITH A MEMBRANE OF YOMA ENERGY...
...SO I CAN SENSE EVERY MOVEMENT, EVEN OUTSIDE MY FIELD OF VISION.

AH... THAT'S HOW RAFAELA FOUGHT.
I HAVE RECEIVED RAFAELA'S MEMORIES AND EMOTIONS.

SLASH
SLASH
SLA
SH
GA
SSH

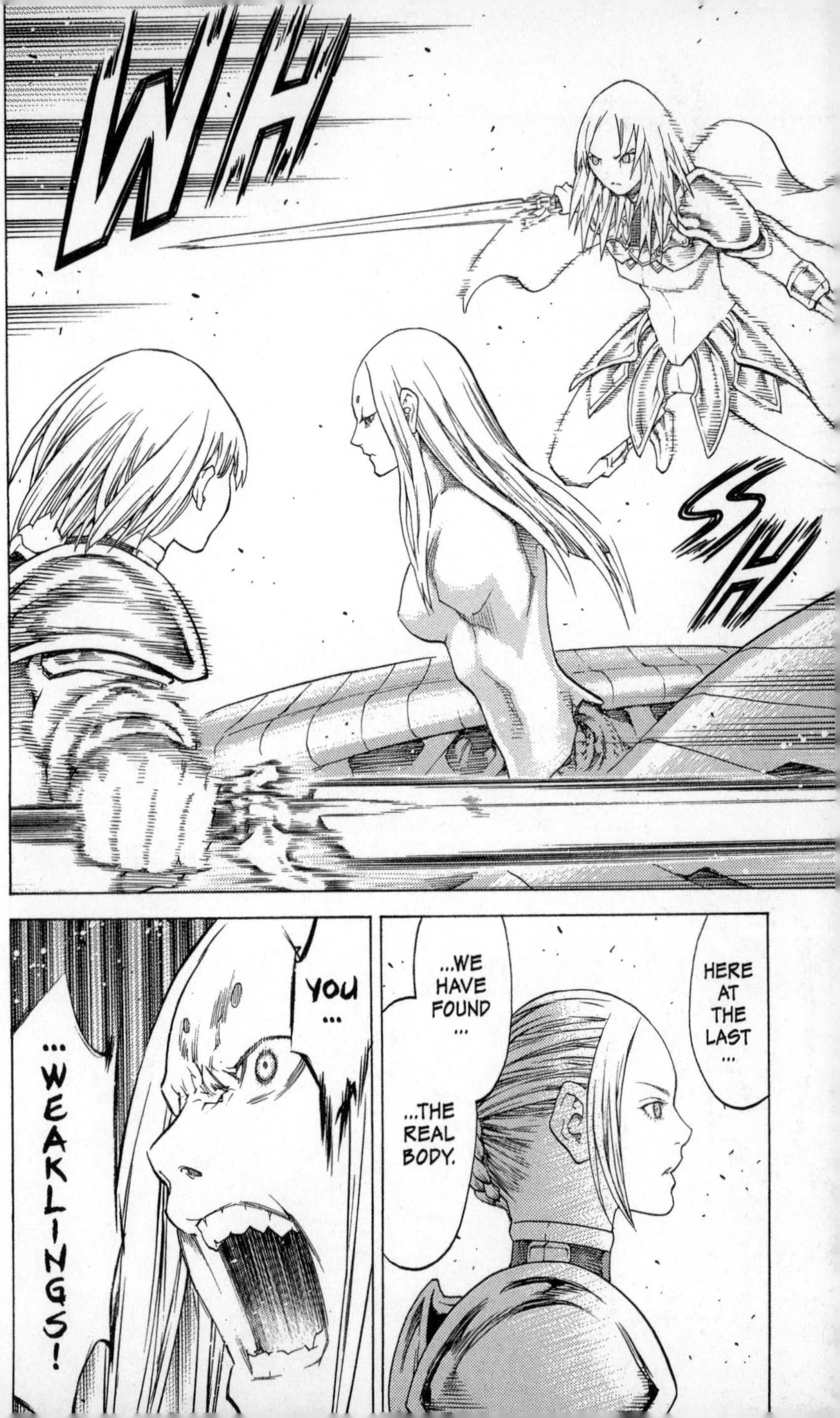

HERE AT THE LAST ...
...WE HAVE FOUND ...
...THE REAL BODY.
YOU ...
...WEAKLINGS!

DO

SHU

GA

DAMN!
THEY'VE ALREADY TAKEN DOWN THEIRS!
AND WE'VE GOT SIX WARRIORS! WE'RE PITIFUL!

ITS STRUCTURE IS SIMPLE, SO I THOUGHT THIS WOULD BE EASY...
...BUT IT'S TOUGHER AND FASTER THAN I THOUGHT.

GO

GA

SHU

BIKI
BIKI
BIKI

BOKO
BOKO
BOKO

GISHI
MOST DIFFICULT OF ALL IS ITS REGENER-ATION.
WE NEED A SINGLE SLASHING ATTACK STRONG ENOUGH TO DESTROY A MASSIVE BODY.

BIKI
BIKI
BIKI

READ THIS WAY

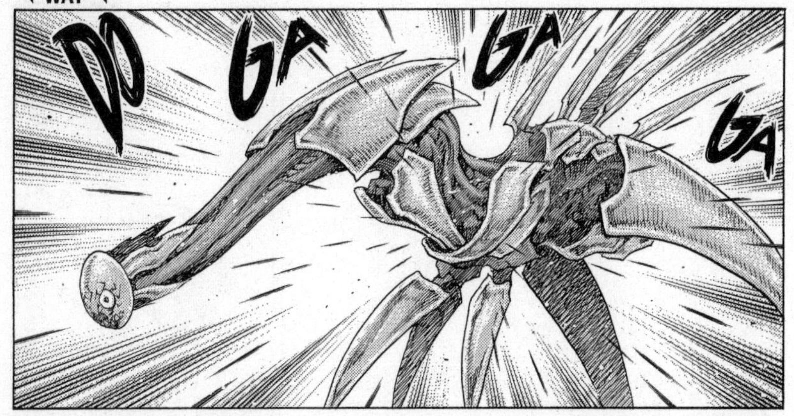
DO
GA
GA
GA

YOUR ATTACKS ARE SO OBVIOUS!
YOU'LL NEVER HIT ME THAT ...

GRAAAAH!

URK
!!

I WON'T LET YOU DESTROY THE HOLY CITY ANY FURTHER ...
...SO I'M STOPPING YOU FOR A SECOND.

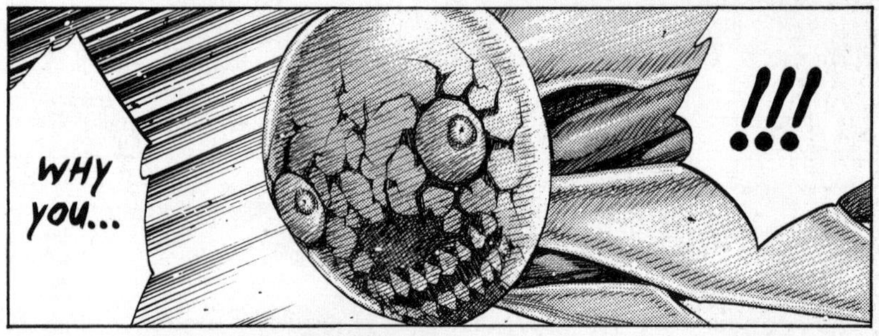
!!!
WHY YOU...

GO!
DAMN ...
...YOU!
GA

GYU
DO
GA

THAT WAS PRISCILLA...
THE AWAKENED BEING CLARE RISKED HER LIFE TO GET REVENGE ON...

BACK IN THE WEST, IN LAUTREC, PRISCILLA SAID SHE SMELLED SOMETHING ON ME...
...AND WAS SEARCH-ING FOR THE SOURCE.

SHE MUST HAVE MEANT CLARE.
BUT WHY? I UNDERSTAND WHY CLARE WOULD SEARCH FOR PRISCILLA, BUT WHY WOULD PRISCILLA LOOK FOR CLARE?

READ THIS WAY

O O O O

 END OF VOL. 23: MARK OF THE WARRIOR

クレイモア

Claymore

VIZMANGA

Read manga anytime, anywhere!

From our newest hit series to the classics you know and love, the best manga in the world is now available digitally. Buy a volume* of digital manga for your:

- iOS device (**iPad®, iPhone®, iPod® touch**) through the **VIZ Manga app**
- Android-powered device (**phone or tablet**) with a browser by visiting **VIZManga.com**
- **Mac or PC computer** by visiting **VIZManga.com**

VIZ Digital has loads to offer:

- 500+ ready-to-read volumes
- New volumes each week
- FREE previews
- Access on multiple devices! Create a log-in through the app so you buy a book once, and read it on your device of choice!*

To learn more, visit www.viz.com/apps

*** Some series may not be available for multiple devices. Check the app on your device to find out what's available.**

viz.com/apps

You're Reading in the Wrong Direction!!

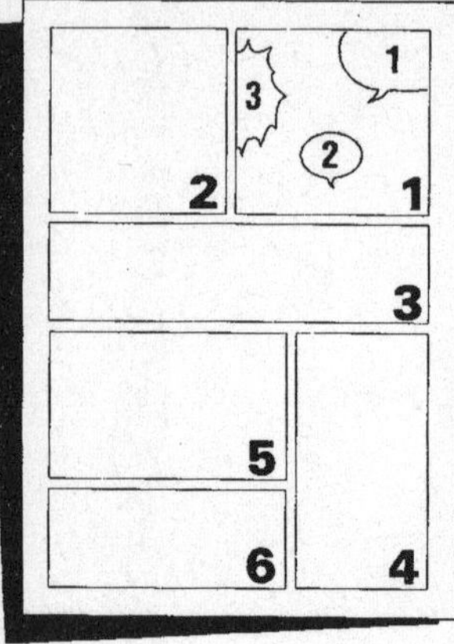

Whoops! Guess what? You're starting at the wrong end of the comic!

...It's true! In keeping with the original Japanese format, **Claymore** is meant to be read from right to left, starting in the upper-right corner.

Unlike English, which is read from left to right, Japanese is read from right to left, meaning that action, sound effects and word-balloon order are completely reversed... something which can make readers unfamiliar with Japanese feel pretty backwards themselves. For this reason, manga or Japanese comics published in the U.S. in English have sometimes been published "flopped"—that is, printed in exact reverse order, as though seen from the other side of a mirror.

By flopping pages, U.S. publishers can avoid confusing readers, but the compromise is not without its downside. For one thing, a character in a flopped manga series who once wore in the original Japanese version a T-shirt emblazoned with "M A Y" (as in "the merry month of") now wears one which reads "Y A M"! Additionally, many manga creators in Japan are themselves unhappy with the process, as some feel the mirror-imaging of their art skews their original intentions.

We are proud to bring you Norihiro Yagi's **Claymore** in the original unflopped format. For now, though, turn to the other side of the book and let the adventure begin...!

—Editor